Mahatma Gandhi
And
The New Millennium

Mahatma Gandhi
And
The New Millennium

By

Dr. M. Maharajan,

M.A., Ph.D., D. Litt., LL. B.,

School of Gandhian Thought and
Development Studies
Mahatma Gandhi University
Kottayam–686 560
Kerala

DISCOVERY PUBLISHING HOUSE
New Delhi

First Published – 2001
Reprinted-2011
ISBN 81-7141-603-

Published by :
DISCOVERY PUBLISHING HOUSE
4831/24, Ansari Road, Prahlad Street,
Darya Ganj, New Delhi-110002 (INDIA)
☎ : 3279245 • Fax : 91-11-3253475
E-mail : dphtemp@indiatimes.com

Mehra Offset Press
Delhi

Preface

The purpose of this book is to analyse how far Gandhiji's ideas and his principles are relevant to the New Millennium.

As the clock struck the midnight hour and church bells chimed, ships hooted and Sirens rent the dark night with unwanted frenzy, the groups of people clustered together at home, hotel, resort, in street corners, plazas in churches and auditoria burst into applause, shook hands, embraced each other and cheered the advent of the new year. It was also the start of the New Millennium and the blocking of another one thousand years in the nation's history. Whether the old Millennium ended or it was the beginning of the new one the night gave way today (1-1-2000) in its eternal routine and nature gave no special indication of it. At the break of down mankind burst out into a Universal for a better tomorrow.

On 24th December 1999 an Indian Airlines Air Bus with 187 passengers and eight crew members were hijacked while on a flight from Kathmandu to New Delhi. Through non-violent way negotiations went on with the hijackers and through Gandhian lines all hostages were released by the hijackers on 31-12-1999. So, in the New Millennium Gandhian principles is one of the best principles for solving all problems. Gandhiji's main aim was "The moral regeneration of human society" in which peace can be obtained. Peace begins with a harmony between individuals. Gandhiji lived and worked for the establishment of such relationship among individuals and groups are discussed in the first chapter.

The purpose of second chapter is to analyse Gandhian approach to World Peace. World Peace is an epithet that is on the lips of all right thinking men. But it has become an elusive concept. Tall talks on the need for world peace and the unrelenting pilling up of armaments go on side by side to the bewilderment of sane men.

The problem of world peace has both a negative and a positive aspect. Negatively it involves eradication of war on its positive side peace is no mere cessation of war. Science has made the world "one" and peace in this context denotes an era of positive good will and co-operation among all the countries of the world, so that the whole human race may enjoy a fuller and richer life and derive full advantage from modern science. Gandhiji has often been described as an apostle of peace. He strove and died for peace. Gandhiji advocated peace—but not any price, for his philosophy was a philosophy of commitment.

In the third chapter an attempt is made to analyse the concept of Freedom, Equality and Peace with Gandhian perspective. Gandhiji believed in human freedom and denounced all kinds of suppression. He believed that the ideal society of his conception should be an "ordered anarchy." Such a society would carry the ultimate value on non-violence, freedom, equality and social equilibrium.

In the fourth chapter an attempt is made to analyse Modern Social Legislation. Social Legislation is that which serves the present social and economic objectives of the nation and deals adequately with current social problems. Social legislation is very comprehensive and may include legislation affecting social customs like infanticide, sati, sacrifices and child marriage etc.

In the fifth chapter an attempt is made to analyse Gandhi's approach to communal harmony. Gandhi's approach to communal harmony has a meaning, a worth and is meaningful step in the proper direction but this single step should not be considered as a panacea or a single pill or tablet course for the eradication of a serious disease of communalism.

In the sixth chapter an attempt is made to analyse the concept of child welfare in Gandhi's view. The child welfare is important for the child himself, for the family and for the society. It is important for the child himself in the sense that he will be able to perform his duties well, when he has a good physique, a good mind and a good personality. Gandhian approach to child- and-youth welfare is also based on the recognition of stages of psychological and physical development and of different needs of age groups.

In the seventh chapter an attempt is made to analyse the Concept Women's Welfare in Gandhi's view. Gandhian approach to women's welfare is not so much a protest against a denial of specific rights example – of property or of occupation against this or that particular social evil or as an underlying resentment against social injustice as such directed towards restoration of women to her natural and rightful place in society as an equal rights of man. Gandhiji recognises the equal rights of woman with man irrespective of any disability associated with here name. Gandhiji considered women as the incarnation of Ahiṁsā.

In the eighth chapter an attempt is made to analyse the relevance of Gandhian thought in the New Millennium. The relevance and the application of Gandhian ideas to the present problems of our economy and economic planning have become particularly more significant today with the objective of attaining social justice, eradication of poverty, unemployment, reducing of social and economic inequalities, creating better opportunities for the weaker sections of the society, the small farmers and the landless labourers.

In the concluding chapter some of the important questions are put forth :

1) Have we ever thought to develop our society on Gandhian lines?

2) Are we really moving in that direction?

3) Are we thinking on those lines and trying to help the masses?

4) Are our leaders or rulers leading us in that direction?

5) Do we have equality of opportunity available to all the countrymen?

6) Are the rich class of the society or businessman following the concept of trusteeship in practice?

7) Do we find morality, virtues, good, values etc. being practised by us and are they reigning supreme over the vices and sins?

8) De we have that kind of economic thinking or policies as were advocated by Gandhiji which would have been most beneficial for the teeming masses living?

In the New Millennium if we are able to live according to the ideals of Mahatma Gandhi we may be sure that this country of ours will survive, as it has survived for centuries for many more centuries and its philosophy will make a healing of nations and bringing of people together.

There remains for me a pleasant duty for acknowledgements. My thanks are due to Dr. A.K. Chirappanath, Prof. and Director, School of Gandhian Thought and Development Studies, Mahatma Gandhi University, Kottayam who provided me an opportunity to write this book.

I thank my parents Shri. M. Marimuthu and Smt. M. Thayammal for the blessings showered on me while writing this book.

I thank my wife and daughter Smt. M. Kuttiamma and Kum. M. Preethi Thayammal who gladly took upon themselves the arduous responsibility of seeing the entire matter and also for their helpful suggestions during the final stage of the book.

I am extremely thankful to Sri. Mathew P.V., Vikas Institute, Kumaranalloor, Kottayam, for the excellent computer setting done by him to complete this book.

I would like to thank Discovery Publishing House, New Delhi, for the neat execution of their printing. Last, but not least, my thanks, go out to the Managing Director, Discovery Publishing house, New Delhi who agreed to publish my book. It is my hope that this book will prove to be useful for study and research, especially in the field of Gandhian Thought.

Dr. M. MAHARAJAN

I would like to thank [illegible] New Delhi, for the real encourage[illegible] but not least, my thanks [illegible] to the [illegible] Publishers, [illegible] Delhi who [illegible] book. [illegible] hope that this book will prove to [illegible] and [illegible], especially in the field of Carnatic [illegible]

[illegible]

Contents

List of Abbreviations

A.B.S.S.S	:	Akhil Bharatiya Sarva Seva Sangh, Varanasi
A.I.V.I.A	:	All India Village Industries Annual
A.P.H.	:	Asia Publishing House
B.V.B.	:	Bharatiya Vidyabhavan, Bombay
N.P.H.	:	Navajivan Publishing House, Ahmedabad
P.D.	:	Publications Division, Government of India, New Delhi
S.A.A.	:	Sri. Aurobindo Ashram, Pondicherry
S.P.	:	Sarvodaya Prachuralaya, Tanjore
S.S.S.	:	Sarva Seva Sangh, Varanasi
S.S.S.P.	:	Sarva Seva Sangh Prakashan

Chapter—I

Gandhi and the New World Order

LORD, THOU has been our refuge from one generation to another. Before the mountains were brought forth, or ever the earth and the world made;

Thou art God

From everlasting and world without end.

Thou turnest man to destruction; again thou sayest

Come again, Ye children of men

For a thousand years in thy sight are but as yesterday:

Seeing that is past as a watch in the night.[1]

As the clock struck the midnight hour and church bells chimed, ships hooted and sirens rent the dark night with unwanted frenzy, the groups of people clustered together at home, hotel, resort, in street corners, plazas, in churches and auditoria burst into applause, shook hands, embraced each other and cheered the advent of the New Year. It was also the start of the New Millennium and the blocking of another one thousand years in the nation's history. A Millennium is but a speck in the infinite continuum of time but for the inhabitants of the planet Earth in the contemporary era seeking any possible means to relieve the monotony of a humdrum existence, it is a once-in-a life time event, their mortality reminding them of the fact that they will not be able to witness its passage again!

Whether the old Millennium ended or it was the beginning of the new one the night gave way today in its eternal routine and Nature gave no special indication of it. At the break of dawn, mankind burst out into a Universal Prayer for a better tomorrow. The sun rose this morning (1-1-2000) without much ado and the natural phenomenon could care least how we poor mortals went gaga over a cleverly orchestrated event which read a special significance into an inexorable fact of the wheels of Time grinding, slowly but surely. The Ramans and Ramanujans still hold sway in their respective spheres while Tagore, Ray and the Mahatma are the acknowledged universal icons of Art, Cinema and Statemanship. Let the good time roll out and uncork the bubblies, and the new millennium lead us to peace and prosperity on Gandhian Lines.

World is today faced with a variety of difficult and intricate problems. The Modern military weapons have become so indiscriminate and their effects so catastrophic that the very existence of mankind is threatened. On 24th December 1999 an Indian Airlines air bus with 187 passengers and eight crew members was hijacked while on a flight from Kathmandu to New Delhi. The hijacked plane landed at Lahore tonight after the five heavily armed hijackers killed one passenger during a 25-minute refuelling halt at Amritsar Airport. Pakistani troops and police surrounded the wide-bodied A-300 aircraft when it landed shortly after forcing the pilot Captain D. Saran to take off from Amritsar, having permitted him earlier to land for refuelling. The hijackers demanded food and fuel at the Lahore airport and were insisting on refuelling of the plane to leave for an undisclosed destination, officials said.

The identity of the hijackers who are armed with AK-47 rifles, pistols and hand grenades, was not known nor did they make any demands. They spoke Hindustani and said they wanted to go to their homeland without elaborating. Unconfirmed reports said the four passengers were shot dead while the plane was on the runway at Amritsar's Raja Sansi Airport for 25 minutes on 24-12-1999 after landing there at 6.57 p.m. The circumstances under which the passengers were killed were not clear. One version said the hijackers not angry when the refuelling was stopped but according to another report they got suspicious when an oil tanker moved towards the plane. Of the passengers on board the aircraft 152 are Indians and 24 foreigners, including eight Nepalese, four each Swiss and Spanish and one each Canadian and Belgian. There are 106 men, 57 women, 11 children and two infants on board the plane. Of the 11 members crew, eight are air hostesses.

Pakistani authorities who had earlier refused permission to the aircraft to land at Lahore air it to fly to Amritsar as it was short on fuel, permitted the plane to land on its second attempt after Indian authorities requested them to let the aircraft land. The aircraft made a forced landing after circling over the airport several times. The tarmac lights were switched off when it touched down. In New Delhi, the crisis management group of the union cabinet met tonight (24-12-1999) to discuss the situation. The meeting, presided over by our Hon'ble Prime Minister, Mr. Atal Behari Vajpayee and attended by senior cabinet members Messrs. L.K. Advani, Yashwant Sinha, Jaswant Singh, Pramod Mahajan and Sharad Yadav is taking place at the Prime-Minister's residence.

The Prime Minister's Principal Secretary, Mr. Brajesh Mishra who emerged from the meeting said, "The hijackers obviously belonged to a terrorist outfit."[2] According to Brajesh Mishra said that "at present the pilot Capt. D.Saran is the sole channel of communication."[3] Earlier Capt. D. Saran, informed the control tower at Amritsar that the hijackers had short dead four passengers, according to the airport director Mr. Mulekar. This was confirmed in New Delhi by the Civil Aviation Secretary Shri. Ravindra Gupta, who also said that the plane had take off thereafter with only a few minutes of fuel in it. Most officials have put the number of hijackers at five but others said there were seven of them. Nothing was immediately known about their identity. According to Pakistani authorities the hijackers had demanded medical help and drinking water. Meanwhile Mr. Ravindra Gupta has said that the fact that the hijackers had demanded medical help, indicated that there might be injured people on board. While the Pakistani authorities may supply water and medical facilities, they would not be inclined to refuel the plane as that would enable it to leave Lahore. Mr. Gupta said, we have decided to suspend flights to Kathmandu till "we reassure ourselves of the security arrangements there".

On 26th December 1999 hijackers released 26 passengers from the flight which has been flown to Kandahar, Afganistan. The hijackers demanded for a $ 200 million ransom and the body of Sajjad Afghani a Harkat -Ul-Ansar leader and the hijackers sticking to their demand that 36 militants be freed from Indian Jails. The U.N. officials also had a talk with hijackers, Indian diplomat and other officials from India had negotiations with hijackers. The week long hostage crisis ended on 31st December 1999 when the Vajpayee Government agreed to release (at least) three hard core "Kashmiri" terroists in exchange for the freedom of 155 Indian passengers and the crew members of the hijacked Indian Airlines air craft. All the hostages returned home on 31 12-1999 from Kandahar to freedom and the new millennium— and to an emotional reunion with their loved ones at the Palam airport. It was full efforts taken by our Hon'ble Prime Minister Shri. Atal Behari Vajapyee and Hon'able External Minister Shri. Jasawant Singh. Through non-violent way negotiations went on with the hijackers and through Gandhian lines, i.e., through ahimsa the above problem was solved smoothly. So, in the new millennium Gandhian principles is one of the best principles for solving all problems.

The modern military weapons have become so indiscriminate and their efforts so catastrophic that the very existence of mankind is threatened. Unscrupulous pursuit of material welfare without heading ethical and human values, has eaten into the very vitals of national life and culture. The moral fibre of the people has been weakened. The only practical way to resolve these problems in a lasting manner is to turn once again to the ideals of Mahatma Gandhi, study them in depth and find proper solutions for our ailments. No shadow of doubt can exist that the world needs Gandhiji in the new millennium more than ever before. He is not a relic of the past, but a prophet of the future. In his own words, "So, long as my faith burns bright as I hope it will even if I stand alone, I shall be alive in the grave and what is more, speaking from it."[4] Gandhi's ideas are by no means out moded as some believed, and on the contrary might well be applied more often in today's world.

The Central Principles of Gandhian Thought on economics, politics, social reform and prove their relevance to "THE NEW WORLD ORDER." The relevance of Gandhian ideas, and their universal applicability is precisely because of the fact that his ideas and thoughts are not based on colonial dominations and exploitative attitudes, cut throat competition, and some other material and worldly values. As against these they are based on strong human values with moral and spiritual touching. He wanted to give a spiritual touch to all economic, social, political and other problems which he thought as the root cause of all prosperity and happiness. His ideas were always to the best interests and to the real solution of the problems of man kind.

Mahatma Gandhi stood for a simple and, more or less, self-sufficient living in the rural surroundings mainly because he could foresee that a highly sophisticated and centralised life in the cities would inescapably lead to the organisation of inhuman violences and aggressive nationalism resulting in international tensions and wars of unprecedented devastation. Gandhiji therefore advocated the establishment of ideal villages where the people could pursue the ideal of "simple living and high thinking." But this ideal has been criticised, ridiculed and even denounced as an opiate to keep the poor quiet and help the present social order to go on.

Prof. Dennish Meadow's is of the opinion that human environment is a shocking way and there is limit to the world material growth and the world economy faces a very gloomy picture in the new millennium if we do not change radically our present policies. The indiscriminate use of technology and the pursuance of industrialisation on competitive basis have led to serve economic and social consequences of new and different nature. The ever widening gap between rich and poor, worsening economic and political relations, economic imperialism, multinationals and technostructure are among the more important problems at both the internal and international levels, the solution of which is not becoming possible through the traditional and conventional methods of modern world. With reference to these problems the relevance of Gandhian ideas are very much emphasised by Prof. Tinbergin in the following words – "the rich of the earth should prepare themselves for the simpler life in future. The leading philosophy of the present day society which always asks for more material goods and does not attach much value at simplicity of life or modesty in claims has to be replaced by alternative philosophies and surely much could be learned from Mahatma Gandhi's words and example. The real values of life do contain a sufficient quantity of goods and shelter, but it is not necessary to have the luxuries now aimed at. Cultural values will have to be upgraded again".[5]

According to Gandhiji advancement, is not only economic or industrial it is the ethical and spiritual progress of man's nobler pursuits for a higher and sublimer goal of life. Gandhiji Says, "Civilisation in the real sense of the term consists not in the multiplication, but in the delibrate and voluntary restriction of wants."[6] Even the Laws of diminishing utility and the law of Insatiable wants clearly indicate that the more a man has the less he is able to derive pleasure from the articles of consumption.... The end consists in the total elimination of all the wants, existing at the moment". Just a few months before his death Gandhiji wrote to Mr. Nehru: "The New Social Order that we envisage should not be judged by the quantity of material comforts and luxuries that we are able to accumulate, by the high standard of moral and ethical values that govern the life of a nation."[7] He advised simplification of the standards of living and that one should place voluntary limits on his property and practice self renunciation. Gandhiji held that "many of the so called comforts of life are not only indispensable but positive hinderances to the elevation of mankind."[8] Having correctly diagnosed the disease, he called for the revival of village economy with indigenous industries so that the people could have enough to eat and keep the wolf off their doors.

Chesterton's article was an attack on the so called Indian awakening. His objection was not against Indians asking for independence or preserving their cultural heritage. His objection was against Indians asking for Western political system, education, philosophy etc. He wrote "The right of the people to express itself to be itself in action, was a genuine right. Indians have a right to be and live as Indians. But Herbert Spencer is not an Indian, his philosophy is not Indian philosophy; all his clatter about the science of education and other things is not Indian ... . But this is our first difficulty that Indian nationalist is not national.[9] As Bell rang an alarm on an earlier occasion, Chesterton's words acted as red signal. These words told Gandhiji where to stop and how to proceed. These words were ringing in his mind when he embarked the Kildonan castle on November 13, 1909. Though cool winds were cooling his body, the five of patriotism was smouldering within. There was the clash of ideas and ideals within. There was also the clash between the biting cold, literally and figuratively, outside and the burning five inside. This dialectical conflict brought about an awakening. Indian Home Rule or Hind Swaraj was Gandhi's answer to Chesterton. Dr. Chandran Devanesan calls it the "Manifesto of Gandhian Revolution."[10] No one could now say that Indian nationalist were not national enough.

Indian Home Rule or Hind Swaraj[11] was the product of Gandhiji's profound concern for the welfare of all. It was this concerned that prompted him to wage a relentless non-violent war in South Africa against racial discrimination and resultant injustice. Though Gandhiji's immediate aim was the attainment of true Swaraj for India his ultimate goal was the Swaraj of all mankind. Through the service of India, Gandhiji wanted to serve the whole mankind. By the establishment of Swaraj Gandhiji envisaged the possibility of a new world order, where Truth, Non-violence and Love would be the guiding principles in the relation between man and man and between State and State. Gandhiji wanted India to give lead to the world in this matter.

According to Gandhiji the root meaning of Swaraj being self-rule, it may be rendered as disciplined rule from within, and purna swaraj means completely disciplined Self-rule.[12] He makes a fine distinction between Swaraj and independence. Independence may mean Licence to do as you like.[13] Swaraj is positive, independence is negative.[14] The word Swaraj is a sacred word, a vedic word, meaning self-rule and self-restraint and not freedom from all, restraint which independence often means.[15]

Gandhiji often interchanges the words Swaraj and Ramarajya. Of course Swaraj is the basis of Ramarajya. Ramarajya is the harmonious co-existence of persons who have attained self-control or Swaraj. Ramarajya is not possible without Swaraj. If true Swaraj or Purna Swaraj is attained by all, then Ramarajya will be its natural consequence. Gandhiji says Self-Government entirely depends upon our internal strength, upon our ability to fight against the heaviest odds. Indeed Self-Government which does not require that continuous striving to attain it and to sustain it, is not worth the name. I have, therefore, endeavoured to show both in words and indeed that political Self-Government—that is Self-Government for a large number of men and women—is no better than individual Self-Government and therefore, it is to be attained by precisely the same means that are required for individual self-Government or Self-rule".[16] Again Gandhiji says that "real Swaraj will come out by the acquisition of authority by a few but by the acquisition of the capacity by all to resist authority when abused. In other words Swaraj is to be attained by educating the masses to a sense of their capacity to regulate and control authority."[17] The Swaraj of Gandhiji's dream recognised no racial or religious distinction. It was to be for all. A state where non-violence and love reign supreme, where everyone works according to one's capacity and consumes according to one's needs keeping in mind the welfare of all, would have attained Swaraj for the individuals and Ramarajya for all. This is what the Westerners call the Kingdom of God on earth. Gandhiji preferred to use the words Ramarajya probably because his "Swadeshism" or because the words of Chesterton were still ringing in his mind.

Ramarajya in the narrow Hindu context could mean the rule of Rama, the divine King. But it was not in this sense that Ramarajya was significant. For Gandhiji Rama was not merely a king. He is simply God. Ramarajya then means the Kingdom of God. Ramarajya is significant in another sense also. Rama's rule was an enlightened one. It was true Swaraj when true democracy prevailed, though it was in the forum of a monarchy. Gandhiji calls Ramarajya as the dharmarajya, the rule of dharma. It is also called People's Raj or democracy. As all are children of God, it is only natural that everyone should receive a fair deal.

Gandhiji knew that the welfare of all, which was the ideal of Ramarajya, depended on the moral conviction of the members of Ramarajya, depended on the moral conviction of the members of Ramarajya. This is why he insisted that moral values should guide all our actions. Gandhiji never wanted economics, or politics of religion or morality or any other worthwhile human concern to be kept apart from the other. All have to be mutually supporting and enhancing the value of life. For him politics bereft of religion is absolute dirt, ever to be shunned.[18] " That economics is untrue which ignores or disregards moral values."[19] True economics never militates against the highest ethical standard, just all true ethics to be worth the name, must at the same time be also good economics.[20] His Ramarajya is a moral Kingdom where truth, love and respect for everything being are of supreme importance.

Eventhough Gandhiji insisted on the importance of moral principles in his Ramarajya, he was not unaware of the importance of other factors in the attainment of human welfare. He also knew that man being physical, spiritual and social being all his needs corresponding to these natures should be satisfied atleast in reasonable measure before he could be asked to be happy and contented. Ignoring any one in favour of the others not only does not lead to human welfare and social harmony but leads to political disharmony and distrust. He realised that a "Starving man thinks first of satisfying his hunger than anything else. We will sell his liberty and all for the sake of getting a morsel of food. For them liberty, God and all such words are merely letters but together without the slightest meaning. They jar upon them. If we want to give these people a sense of freedom, we shall have to provide them with work which they can easily do in their desolate homes and which would give them a bare living."[21] Gandhiji understood that economic equality is the master key to non-violent independence[22] and hence a very important aspect of his Ramarajya. He thought that by a few simple principles some kind of practicable economic equality would be achieved.

Gandhiji favoured "production by the masses" opposed to "mass production". But it is significant that he never opposed machinery as such: What he opposed was craze for machinery. Gandhiji was realist; he knew that every country needs certain large-scale industries to cater to vital needs-steel, cement and so on. He knew that even millions of blacksmiths cannot replace a steel plant. But according to him, such industries should be controlled and managed by the State and should occupy the least part of the vast national activities which will mainly be in the villages."[23]

Gandhiji's plan of production by the masses also has other distinct advantages over mass production. As Dr. Schumacher wrote, "The system of mass production, based on sophisticated, highly capital intensive, high energy-input dependent, and human labour—saving technology presupposes that you are already rich, for a great deal of capital investment, is needed to establish one single work place. The system of production by the masses moblises the priceless resources which are possessed by all human beings, their clever brains and skilful hands, and supports them with first-class tools. The technology of mass production is inherently violent, ecologically damaging, self defeating in terms of non-renewable resources, and stultifying for the human person. The technology of mass production by the masses, making use of the best of modern knowledge and experience is conducive to decentralisation, compatible with the laws of ecology, gentle in its use of scarce resources, and designed to serve the human person instead of making him the servant of machines."[24]

For a moment, let us take it for granted that the total output under mass production is larger than that under the system of production by the masses; even the latter should be preferred over the former from the view point of distributional aspect. Gandhiji remarked, "Granting for the moment that machinery may supply all needs of humanity, still it would concentrate production in particular areas, so that you have to go in a round-about way to regulate distribution both in the respective areas where things are required, it is automatically regulated and there is less chance for fraud and none for speculation." It is worth nothing that vast organisations like the General Motors Corporation of the United States and the British National Coal Board have been decentralised to improve efficiency and promote employee's welfare and job satisfaction. Gandhiji's view on the social responsibility of business and his trusteeship theory constitute a revolutionary step in the field of socio-economic reform.

Absence of peace is both the cause and effect of tension in the social, national and international spheres. It frustrates all attempts at economic development, social progress and human solidarity. Inspite of several efforts made by League of Nations and U.N.O. for co-operation and goodwill in the world, the battles have still been going on and a wave of cold war has swept over the world which has created a suffocating atmosphere.

Recently, on 24th December 1999 at Kandahar, Indian Airlines Air Bus was hijacked and 187 passengers were made as hostages. After the information, the U.N.O. officials rushed to Kandahar, Afghanistan and they had a talk with hijackers and at last the U.N.O. talk was failed. The hijackers never accepted the demand made by the U.N.O.officials.

No where peace is found. The race for armament is still going on. The U.N.O. recognises that the Government of almost all the countries of the world are not prepared to renounce war for one reason or the other. War cannot produce peace. It produces only war. One cannot expect peace from the balance of power since it nourishes mutual hatred, struggle for widening the sphere of influence, fear and suspicion, which may be the elements of generating wars. Hence some new and basic thought will have to be adopted for permanent and long lasting world peace.

Gandhiji an apostal of non-violent action never approved war—a violent action. He rejected outright and condemned war as a means of resolving a conflict. According to Gandhi the problem of peace was not just a political problem involving the adjustment or rectification of relations between armed nations. It was the problem of mankind, posing a challenge not only to states but also to every individual human being and human group. He, therefore, endeavoured to established peace between man and man, group and group and nation and nation.

It was a life long conviction with Gandhiji that mankind and its civilisation can be saved from destruction only through non violence. The individual as well as his environment—local, national and international have to be purged of violence. If the individual regenerates himself—through strict self-discipline, and if the nations of the world reconstruct themselves along non-violent lines, the emerging international order will naturally be peaceful and co-operative. The great fear of a war and destruction could at once disappear. Indeed the adoption and practice of such an idea at global level is an urgent need of the day. Such a condition could avert the modern wars which have the potentiality to cause unimaginable horrors and destruction not once to the present generation but also to the coming generations. At the very outset one finds that his approach to the problem of world peace was overloaded with moral philosophy of life. It is for this reason that the Mahatma had been scoffed at by many of his critics as an utopian, blind to the facts of the grim world of real politics. At the same time one has to be cautious while challenging Gandhian philosophy of life and his techniques of action. Gandhiji's main aim was the "moral regeneration of human society" in which peace can be obtained. One has to take into account that moral philosophy does play an important role in the relation of human behaviour. In the same way the application of moral values in regulating the behaviour of nations is also possible. George Caltin, one of the important political scientists, is of the opinion that "the mission of Mahatma Gandhi was to be our educator, and to call the world's attention on the need for an education in the beauties of Ahimsa."[25]

Gandhiji advised us to mobilise millions of people for non-violent resolution of conflicts and for the proper achievement and establishment of world peace. This would mean the adoption of the following ways:

a) "Starting a non-violent movement on the international level. Peace worker all over the world must unite.

b) Through peace education workers should bring a change in mentality of the masses and infuse the feeling of unity."

Peace workers of each nation should press their government for total disarmament which requires a strong public opinion. So long as total disarmament is not accepted atleast nations should not join military pacts.

It would not be out of place to mention that apart from his own philosophy of peace, Gandhiji also advocated certain other measures such as disarmament, world peace organisation and world police to secure peace. Gandhiji suggested disarmament. In his own words Gandhiji says that "real disarmament cannot come unless the nations of the world cease to exploit one another. If the mad race for armaments continues, it is bound to result in a slaughter such as has never occurred in the history."

Gandhiji further said that, "absence of fundamental sincerity makes all talk about the limitation of armament meaningless. Not disarmament—whether partial or total in respect of nuclear weapons, but renunciation of all force is the answer to the problem of international peace."[26]

Gandhiji suggested that only a world organisation backed by a moral or non-violent sanction can guarantee international peace. He had given his own view regarding the nature of this world organisation different from the nature of the present day U.N.O.

According to Gandhiji this world peace organisation must have the following characteristics:

1. The individuals and the nations composing the world should be predominantly non-violent.
2. All the nations of the world should be fully independent. There can be no place in such a world for colonialism, imperialism and race hatred.
3. The distinction of big and small should be obliterated and every nation should feel as tall as the tallest. Each and every nation must be represented in the International organisation.

4. It should be based on general disarmament. Failing that some one nation, at least, should take the initiative and give a lead to the rest of the world. Its example may become infections in course of time, even as the example of the non-violent individual become infectious.

5. The International Society should be a voluntary organisation of States for the common good, in which every nation should be willing to sacrifice itself for all.

6. All disputes between nations should be settled peacefully and amicably by such methods as negotiation, mediation and arbitration.

As a realist Gandhiji was prepared to concede that "there might be a world police in the absence of universal belief in non-violence"[27] But this force would be, "a concession to human weakness, not ...an emblem of peace."[28] This would function more as a SHANTI SENA or a PEACE BRIGADE than a modern fighting force. The successful implementation of the Gandhian technique depends on the willingness of the individual to commit himself for the chosen ideal with the attitude of "one step is enough to me." His manner of living will indicate his commitment. What he is and does is not without significance. The way to peace lies through peace.

Peace is a relationship between people and between certain kinds of people. Peace begins with a harmony between individuals. Gandhiji lived and worked for the establishment of such relationship among individuals and groups. His is an unique contribution to peace in the modern context. Gandhiji's style of life and the techniques he propounded deserve to be studied and applied so that the world may be a safe place to live. Gandhian ideas were relevant during his life-time, continue to be relevant in the New Millennium and shall remain so for many decades to follow.

Reference:

(1) *"The Hindu"* Saturday, January 1, 2000 - P.1

(2) *"The Hindu"* dated 25-12-1999, P. 1

(3) Ibid – P. 1

(4) *Journal of Gandhian Studies*, University of Allahabad, P. 101.

(5) Jan Tinbergin, *Limit to Growth*, The Economic Times, Annual 1972.

(6) *Economic Thought of Mahatma Gandhi*, ed. J.S. Mathur, P. 612.

(7) *Journal of Gandhian Studies*, University of Allahabad, P. 103.

(8) *Journal of Gandhian Studies*, University of Allahabad, P. 103.

(9) *Mahatma Gandhi, Collected Works*, Vol. IX: PP. 426-27.

(10) C. Devanesan, *The Making of the Mahatma*. P. 364.

(11) *Gandhi, Collected works*, Vol. X. PP. 6-68.

(12) *Ibid*, Vol. XIV. P. 263.

(13) *Ibid*

(14) *Ibid*. P. 264

(15) *Ibid*

(16) N.K. Bose, *Selections from Gandhi*, P. 35.

(17) *Gandhi, Op. Cit.* P. 475.

(18) Sri. Krishnakripala (ed.) *All men are Brothers*, P. 69

(19) *Gandhi, Op.* cit., P. 475.

(20) Bose, *Op. cit.*, P. 40.

(21) *Gandhi, Op. Cit.* XXX, P. 133.

(22) *Journal of Gandhian Studies*, University of Allahabad, P. 95.

(23) *Ibid* – P. 95

(24) *Ibid* – P. 96.

(25) *Ibid* – P. 105.

(26) *Ibid* – P. 106.

(27) *Ibid* – P. 107.

28) *Ibid* – P. 107.

❑ ❑ ❑

Chapter—II

Gandhian Approach to World Peace

The purpose of second chapter is to analyse Gandhian approach to world peace. From the time immemorial there has been a keen desire for peace in human mind. It is true that there have been innumerous wars in the past, but man has always thought in terms of establishing peace in the society, country and the world. Peace as a matter of fact has been a necessary condition for progress. In the 21st century i.e., in the new millennium peace may acquire a new magnitude as the existence of human civilisation itself depends on peace. The world, has become a small family as a result of the extraordinary growth of Science and Technology, but at the same time it has added new dimensions not to violence and destruction. The question facing the humanity today is not to choose between violence and non-violence but to choose between destruction and survival. With star wars at us and the global annual military expenditure nearing the staggering figure of 1000 billion dollars, there has been a growing realisation of the urgent necessity, to abolish wars—either we abolish war or war will abolish us".[1]

World peace is an epithet that is on the lips of all right thinking men. But it has become an elusive concept. Tall talks on the need for world peace and the unrelenting piling up of armaments go on side by side to the bewilderment of sane men. The yawning gap between profession and practice of this score is indeed a disconcerting one. Every time humanity finds itself on the brink of a war, it manages to effect a narrow escape only to find itself again on the brink. Humanity has failed to learn lessons from history. The most tragic part of this episode is while we are quick to discern disaster, we do precious little to cry a halt to it. The choice before humanity today is co-existence or co-extinction.

According to Rev. Martin Luther King : "the choice before mankind is between non-violence and non-existence". It is precisely in this context that the Gandhian approach to world peace comes to acquire a sharp relevance. Rightly, Gandhiji is often associated, with unilateral disarmament. As a messiah of peace and non-violence, he repeatedly asserted the supremacy of moral force over physical force. His advocacy of the use of soul force in preference to physical violence even in the atomic age under scores his strong faith in the spirit of man and the capacity of weak countries to resist aggression from strong ones. Gandhiji has in his armoury weapons to promote world peace even in this nuclear age.

The problem of world peace has both a negative and a positive aspect. Negatively it involves eradication of war. On its positive side, peace is no mere cessation of war. Science has made the world "one", and peace in this context denotes an era of positive goodwill and Co-operation among all the countries of the world, so that the whole human race may enjoy a fuller and richer life and derive full advantage from modern science.

To abolish war, we must get rid of our anger, hate, passion, pride, cupidity, fear, egotism and inordinate ambition and lust for power. We must so reorganise our economic structure as to eliminate exploitation of man by man and of one people by another. There should surely be increase in production, but it must be accompanied by increase in live and sympathy as well. People must also be made to realise that peace has an independent value and should be sought after its own sake.

Nations should abhor war, stop expenditure on armaments and must inculcate international mindedness. Man should be made to feel that he is primarily a human being and not the resident of particular country. He should feel he is a "Universal man" his slogan being "Jai Jagat". (Victory) to the world embraces within its ambit "Jai Hind" (Victory to India) also. Gandhiji has often been described as an apostle of peace. He strove and died for peace. He advocated "peace—but not any price" for his philosophy was a philosophy of commitment. His philosophy of peace is to be differentiated from the conservative plea for peace at any cost. He saw peace as integrally related to justice. Peace is not mere cessation of hostilities. He did not share the diplomatic view of peace. Peace for him meant a positive state of affairs, the pre-condition being freedom from exploitation. In his opinion, only non-violent and just peace could ensure lasting peace.

"Peace will never come until the great powers courageously decide to disarm themselves. Exploitation and domination of one nation over another can have no place in a world striving to put amend to all wars. In such a world only the militarily weaker nations will be free from the fear of intimidation or exploitation. I have no doubt that unless big nations shed their desire of exploitation and the spirit of which war is the natural expression and atombomb the inevitable consequence, there is no hope for peace in the world."[2]

Arbitration, World Government, International Organisation, disarmament and world police and defence force are the traditional solutions suggested for preventing aggression. Gandhiji was no enthusiastic admirer of legal positivism. He had his reservations about the efficacy of international Law as an instrument for the solution of inter-state disputes.

Gandhiji fervently hoped for "a world federation of free and independent state." His concept of World Government transcended the traditional thinking", the pattern of conventional international organisations could not satisfy the conditions for bringing genuine peace. He held that peace could not be established through mere conferences."[3] He was not optimistic about the League of Nations and the U.N. Since they lacked the spirit of non-violence and failed to serve as vehicles of peace in the absence of a force to enforce their decisions.

Gandhiji believed that the doctrine of non-violence held good in the matter of relationship between states and states also. This conviction impelled him to unequivocally recommend total disarmament. He was optimistic enough to advocate unilateral disarmament. "If even one great nation were unconditionally to perform the supreme act of renunciation many of us unconditionally to perform the supreme act of renunciation many of us would see in our life-time visible peace established on earth. His call for unilateral disarmament betrayed his idealism, while the realist Gandhiji appreciated that with the establishment of a democratic world federation disarmament would be practicable in all countries.

Gandhiji believed that disarmament was possible only through "the matchless weapon of non-violence." And it was his hope that "India will ... prove herself worthy of being the first nation in the world to give lead to other nations for the delivery of earth from the burden of war. He wanted the great powers lead the rest by disarming themselves: they should give up ambitions and exploitation and revise their mode of life. Thus according to Gandhiji, disarmament cannot crystallise, unless the nations of the world cease to exploit one another. Exploitation must go ... that is the essential pre-condition for the establishment of a world free from blood-spilling and destruction.

Gandhiji advocated Satyagraha as the sure and potent weapon of combating Inter-state aggression. Satyagraha is universally acceptable. Non-violence, according to him, excludes war and ushers in peace. Gandhiji's ideas about peace suggest that the solution he offered for effecting world peace transcended the frontiers of international diplomacy. The chief limitation of international diplomacy is that it is based up on recognition of the power-system. The Gandhian way claims to stand for non-violent and non-exploitative Social order which alone can ensure just and enduring peace. It may be argued that the Gandhian declarations on peace bristle with some practical difficulties. But Gandhiji would ask that if an individual could practice non-violence why whole nations could not do so. He believed that one must make a beginning and the rest would follow. The Gandhian concept of world peace should be viewed within the general frame work of his philosophy of ahimsa. A proper appreciation of his doctrine of ahimsa would facilitate comprehension of the logical application of that doctrine.

Sceptics consider Gandhian plea for disarmament utopian. In fact, it is not so. Its success depends on the nature of human beings. Gandhiji has great faith in the godliness of human nature." Human nature is essentially peace loving. Even when man fights violently, he does so out of a desire to live in peace. The way of world peace lies in cultivating the spirit of non-violence and peace in the hearts of men. As the individuals are built, so the nations are built. And as the nations are built, so the world is built. Gandhiji says: there is not one law for the atom and another for the universe."

The life-style of Mahatma Gandhi is quite enough to prove that he was able to reduce himself virtually to "the level of the poorest of the poor." As for an ordinary human being, it would be too much to expect what would have been possible for a great man like Gandhi. We must however, have to learn a lesson from Gandhiji's style of living, for as an effective means to achieve Socialism there is no alternative to simple living and noble thinking and this is more so for a developing country like ours.

It goes without saying that a world of peace and prosperity can never be achieved by the use of force. It was Mahatma Gandhi who invented a new weapon that alone could save mankind from a war of total annihilation. Gandhiji and the atombomb were infact "the two originalities of our time and one would defeat the other before it ended".

Jayaprakash Narayan has very aptly said about Mahatma Gandhi that "He was specifically a prophet of the atomic age in which in which the engines of violence which man has invented for the first time in history threaten to destroy the whole of mankind. Gandhiji not only preached non-violence as a Philosophy and an ideal but practised it on a very colossal scale and did it, if not with complete success, with very great success. As long as there is violence which threatens the very future of the human race, the relevance of Gandhiji would continue. Gandhiji will remain relevant till the changes of total annihilation of the human race is removed."

Peace is a relationship between people and between people. Peace begins with a harmony between individuals. Gandhiji lived and worked for the establishment of such relationship among individuals and groups. His is a unique contribution to peace in the modern context. Gandhiji's style of life and the techniques he propounded deserved to be studied and applied so that the world may be a safe place to live.

Gautama Buddha preached the message of Ahimsa and Compassion. Asoka one of the greatest emperors had followed the Buddha's teachings in giving up wars and to tread the path of peace though only after being vexed with the carnage which the Kalinga was had brought about. Jesus Christ whom the Christians worship as the Saviour and Lord is described as the prince of peace. He has lived and preached the message of love, forgiveness and peace. In contemporary times Gandhiji has relentlessly voiced the efficacy of non-violence as against violence.

H.G. Wells in one of his last writings had predicted that man is unfit to live in this world as he knows what is good but does not know how to do good. Man wants peace but does not know how to achieve it. Hence he being incapable of doing what he knows to be the right would destroy himself. The future would show whether H.G. Wells is right or wrong.[4] However, a survey of the contemporary world is ominous. Since has perfected the weapons of war and nations have manufactured and stored them in enough numbers to such an extent that an outbreak of war would not only destroy the living and the products of civilisation, but also would make the surface and atmosphere of the earth uninhabitable for hundreds of years if not for ever. Leaders of nations and man in general are aware of this fact and they dread another war. War is an international nightmare. Man would like to avoid or escape wars if possible.

It is known that Gandhiji is opposed to violence and wars.

Gandhiji is an advocate of non-violence and peace. Though non-violence is "as Old as the hills", Gandhiji's exposition, clarification and forceful advocacy of non-violence is unique. The Gandhian way of peace springs from the basic concept of non-violence.

War is said to be a way of ending wars. As a matter of fact the second world war was fought by the allies with a view to end all wars. Gandhiji is of the firm opinion that war can never end wars. Violence breeds only violence but can never end violence. War is destructive where as peace is constructive. They are two opposite processes. Further violence, being destructive, is a negative process, whereas peace, being constructive, is a positive process. Peace is a positive force of cementing people. War which is a destroying and divisive force can never contribute to the establishment of peace. Hence the search for peace should be in the way of non-violence alone. What Napolean had said to the emperor of Austria in a personal appeal after a fierce battle is worthy of note:

"Thousands of Frenchmen and Austrians have been killed. The prospect of continuance of such horrors distresses me so greatly that I make a personal appeal to you. Amid grief and surrounded by 15,000 corpses, I implore your Majesty, I feel bound to give you an urgent warning. Let us give our generation peace and tranquility. If the men of later days are such fools as to come to blows, they will learn wisdom after a few years of fighting and will then live at peace with one another".

Napolean had sent this appeal for peace at the height of his glory and success. He saw the futility of war to end hostilities and appealed for peace. Napolean subscribed to the Gandhian view when he said, "There are only two powers in the world, those powers are the spirit and the sword. In the long run the Sword will always be conquered by the Spirit."[5]

Gandhi writes, "There will be international league only when all the nations big or small, composing it are fully independent".[6] An International league based on non-violence leads to the establishment of world peace. Such a league implies and it is possible only when it consists of independent nations.

As long as any nation is not independent, there would not be world peace. It is necessary that all nations should be independent to be equal partners in the league of nations in order to have peace.

Gandhiji in adopting non-violent means to get Swaraj for India aimed at achieving international peace by doing so. Gandhiji said, "I suggest to the friends of peace for the world, that the congress in 1920 took a tremendous step towards peace when it declared that it would attain her own, namely Swaraj, by non-violent and truthful means. And I am positive that if we unflinchingly adhere to these means in the prosecution of our goal, we shall have made the largest contribution to the world peace."[7]

According to Gandhi there are certain conditions which are conducive for international peace. They are:

(i) All nations should be independent;

(ii) The equality of all nations should be recognised;

(iii) Disarmament should be accepted by the nations both in principle and their practice.

Wars are the result of lust for power. In some way or other some nations want to establish supremacy over at least some of the other nations. They derive to create and perpetuate inequalities so as to maintain their superiority. Self aggrandisement gives rise to inequality and inequality in return affords scope for self-aggrandisement. It is a vicious circle which can be broken only by an international law by which all nations are treated as equal. The spirit of self-aggrandisement is killed to some extent, though it requires to be more nullified by education, by the proclamation of equality of all nations by an international law. Such a law in the course of time would become a convention and defacto accomplishment. Equality of nations would go a long way- to establish peace in this world.

In the present day world all nations have become independent. Political independence of nations which looked like a mirage and dream has become an actuality. There is still ideological imperialism and also economic domination of one nation over others. Such dependencies also would disappear in course of time. Independence is bound to pave the way for the complete independence and equality of nations.

Is peace the real answer to solve conflicts and violence. The problem arises as to how man can realise peace. According to Toynbee, "The source of peace and war is the interior of life of each individual human spirit." We should not forget that man is the source the centre and purpose of all life. Peace begins in our own hearts. The universality of spirit lies not in knowing much, but in loving extensively. Peace is really the reflection of heaven upon earth. In the Hebrew language, the word "Shalon" means peace with justice. It means inner security and external excess. He will be a man of Peace who has in him the combination of both. Arnold Toynbee espousing the cause of peace observed: "When the pursuit of peace is whole-hearted, it covers every aspect of human affairs.

Today, we live in a violent world. But man fundamentally desires peace. It is recognised by all that no positive civilisation, no just social order or stable peace can flow from violence, war and repression. A true social order must be based, upon persuasion, conviction, and a positive will to co-operation and fellowship among them. These are the only bonds which can hold society together with any permanence and to any real advantage. But because of the differences in world-out look, thinkers, statesmen and politicians differ as to the effective way of establishing just and lasting peace. Gandhiji made singular contribution to the cause of world peace and his views therefore demand close scrutiny.

Gandhiji has often been described as an apostle of peace. Certainly he was. He strove and died for peace. Gandhiji advocated "peace—but not at any price', for his philosophy was a philosophy of commitment—it was based upon the concept of moral responsibility, as well not that of "peace at any price" which under lay his ethic of intention.

Gandhiji's philosophy of peace is to be sharply distinguished from the conservative plea for "Peace at any cost" which is in essence a plea for the maintenance of status quo. Peace, Gandhiji advocated is integrally related to justice. As Gandhiji wrote: "Peace must be just." Peace is not mere cessation of hostilities. Gandhiji did not share the diplomatic view of peace. Peace for him connoted a positive state of affairs, the pre-condition being freedom from exploitation. What he advocated was non-violent and just peace which alone in his opinion, could ensure lasting peace. Gandhiji's ideas about peace suggest that the solution he offered for effecting world peace transcended the frontiers of international diplomacy. The chief limitation of international diplomacy is that it is based upon recognition of the power-system.

The Gandhian way claims to stand for non-violent and non-exploitative social order which alone can ensure just and enduring peace. Non-violence, according to Gandhi, excludes war and ushers in peace.

One may argue that the Gandhian declarations on peace contain some practical difficulties for them to be implemented in the present day world. But Gandhiji would not countenance such a "practical" difficulty. He would counterpoise by saying: "If an individual can practise non-violence, why not whole groups of individuals and whole nations? He believed that one must make a beginning and the rest would follow. The Gandhian concept of world peace should be viewed as in integral part of his philosophy of life and one should try to appreciate his attitude within the general frame work of philosophy of ahimsa. Good means alone can lead us to ever lasting peace. If peace is established by violence it will be of no use. Now a days quite often we read in the newspapers that police, in some places army, marching into an agitating place and peace being established. But that peace is undoubtedly that of the grave yard." But when the non-violent person wins, he wins the heart of the foe.

Gandhiji's concept of peace on earth and goodwill among mankind has lead to the development of Sarvodaya Social order which India's distinctive contribution to world of thought. The application of moral truth to the facts of social life is the essence of Gandhian and Valluvar's way of life. Their dynamic Philosophy can make possible the advent of a radically transformed society. They serve as a system of norms and moral values that can guide our conduct and action in society and state. The truth of a few will count, the untruth of millions will vanish even like a chaff before a whiff of wind. The message of Gandhiji and Tiruvalluvar will remain permanent in the hearts of one and all. Tiruvalluvar really transcends Jesus who only wants to forgive them. In advising to forget the trespasses Valluvar is only in the positive degree. Mahatma Gandhi and Tiruvalluvar have become the symbols of peace, truth, non-violence and dharma. If an individual can practise non-violence, why not whole groups of individuals and whole nations? Gandhiji believed that one must make a beginning and the rest would follow. Gandhian concept of world peace should be viewed as an integral part of his philosophy of life and one should try to appreciate his attitude within the general framework of his philosophy of ahimsā.

Human nature is essentially peace loving. Even when man fights making use of violence he does so, to be able to live in peace. The way of world peace lies in cultivating the spirit of non-violence and peace in the hearts of men.

Reference:

(1) *Journal of Gandhian Studies* Edited by Prof.J.S. Mathur, Institute of Gandhian Thought and Peace Studies, University of Allahabad, P. 106.

(2) *Ibid*—P. 109

(3) *Ibid*—p. 110

(4) *Ibid*—P. 61

(5) *Ibid*—P.62

(6) *Ibid*—P.64

(7) *Ibid*—P.65

❑❑❑

Chapter—III

The Concept of Freedom, Equality and Peace—a Gandhian Perspective

In this chapter an attempt is made to analyse the concept of Freedom, Equality, and Peace in the perspective of Gandhian Thought. Attention is also given to the implications of societal self-direction and to the interrelatedness of personality, culture and society as aspects of social change. The concept of progress is explained here as subjective evaluative aspect of social change. Ideas and ideologies need to be understood as powerful agents in social change. Thus a general foundation is laid for the consideration of change in several institutionalised areas of human behaviour—the economic, political, religious and legal, from the perspective of Gandhian Thought. This study is meant to be objective, realistic and practical, it is also meant to be both positive and constructive.

"Historians of the future, I believe, will look upon this century not as the atomic age; but as the age of Gandhi."[1] observed Prof. Eknath Easwaran at the campus of University of California at Burkley.

Is Mahatma Gandhi the Greatest Man of the age? What was unique in him? How has he achieved this greatness? The questions are natural. To understand Gandhi and his philosophy of life, we would have to look into his life, we would have to discover the Gandhi The Man".

It is almost a new civilisation and culture which Mahatma Gandhi has projected. How much of it can be applicable immediately to the present day problems has to be studied and applied. While intellectual understanding is fundamentally necessary, more important is heartful acceptance of approach and will to act accordingly.

"My life is my message" observed Gandhi. Life reveals all men and death reveals the eminent. This is true in the case of the Mahatma. Gandhi's cherished desire was expressed this: "I wish to wipe every tear from every human eye". He tried to alleviate the sufferings of the sick, the poor and the downtrodden. Inspite of the earnest efforts, he could not succeed to the extent he desired. It was because he lived far ahead of his times and the people could not respond to his mighty moral awakening due to their inherent weakness. It is not necessary to lose hope.

Gandhiji's thought grew with him. He did not deduce system from postulates as conclusion from premises in a syllogism. His concepts are existential and they indicate a development value. The method is heuristic not holistic. He found them in life's tumble of events. He must not fragment his teachings. His thought has grown round a cluster of ideas. They all centre around Truth and Non-Violence.

Gandhiji's passion for Truth, found in every person a divine fire, with a diamond-sharp sincerity, opposed every force which enslaved man, woman or child. The central conviction of man's dignity and divinity flamed forth in many revolutionary articles of faith and spread over the whole spectrum of celestial and terrestrial being in the advaitic spirit. This became his God, that is Truth, his human divine conception, his spiritual orientation, secular toleration and belief in the moral order of mankind his conviction that higher values are basic to politics, economics and other material pursuits, his fascination for Sarvodaya and abjuration of violence his communism without cruelty and government without coercion and his creed that there is innate goodness in every man. And this is the secret of his merger with the hungry, the poor, the sick and the downtrodden. He was a Mahatma because he realised that regardless of station, colour, creed or skin, everyone was at man and any system that dimished or denied this truth was unjust, asuric and ultra vires.

The social philosophy that sustained his life-work and life style was a eclectic and open-minded as Gandhi himself. An open-minded system of social philosophy has one essential characteristic unity of thought and practice. The primacy of this unity was recognised by Gandhi.

Gandhi who did not claim adherence to any set ideology, described his continuing quest in the realms of thought and action as "Experiment with Truth". The thought and practice of Gandhi provides a fruitful area for rethinking, Gandhian ideas present a complete, even if not fully articulated, basis of an entire socio-ethical system. The dynamics of the relationship between Maxim and Truth and the "Welfare of all" and the operational role of non-violence will progressively bring into realisation the commodities of Gandhi's utility function. In short, Gandhi achieved a great change in history, through the application of the principle of Satyagraha. He turned the historic process into a supra-personal fact. Gandhiji presents ethical significance in terms of man's social responsibilities.

Gandhiji's speculative wisdom includes an enquiry into power structure, institutional frameworks, balance between technical skills and spiritual culture, ends and means to deal, with human and historical situation, moral facts in new economic order and a synthesis of individual and Social attitudes. Thus Gandhi drew all human activities into the widening not of philosophy. By asserting its centrality in all levels of thought and action, Gandhi stirs philosophy from its apathy of irrelevance.

Gandhiji was a revolutionary thinker. He revolted wherever the status quo offered a challenge to his conscience. His acceptance of spiritual determinism gave him supreme faith in the inevitable emergence of the non-violent society in the future. The emphasis on spontaneity, faith and devotion, the acceptance of love as the supreme value, the demand for service and sacrifice, the insistence on the dignity of Truth—all these find full manifestation in the life and teachings of Gandhi. He was sanguine that political action would be made to conform to the ultimate values of the spirit.

Gandhij showed to the whole world the efficacy of the principle of live and peace as instrument of social change. His undying faith in the goodness of man and the efficacy of non-violence is beyond doubt. Since the individual is the basis of all social progress, one should place greater reliance on the development of the individual than of any intellectual device. Man is not a "lost" creature. He is ever capable of self-development. The fundamental Gandhian means for bringing about social change rests on the reformation of the individual "internally, morally and spiritually". If all individuals practised self-control, a control over all senses, followed the principles of truth and non-violence in their daily dealings and tried to incorporate these principles in their thoughts and attitudes, society would gradually gravitate towards the ideal he cherished. Essentially, all the teachings of Gandhi, were entirely based on the concept of individual perfection by a strict adherence to Truth and Non-violence.

The world today is in the thores of a new birth. Social philosophy in the East and West, tired of their "isms" and ideologies are eagerly grouping for some new synthesis. In India, at any rate, philosophers are keenly interested to bridge the gulf between tradition and modernity, secular and profane, science and spirituality. They cannot afford to edge nervously from these crucial issues. Gandhiji's message of interpersonal understanding as the only cultured and human method for the solution of problems waxing mankind has to be analysed in depth. The basis of freedom is the dignity of human personality. Every individual by virtue of his humanity, is an end in himself and cannot be regarded only as a means for purpose extraneous to himself. The social institution of family. Marriage, property, education, religion and the state provide the training ground for the individual to develop this personality to the fullest extent. They help an individual to fulfill his basic aspirations of life by submitting himself to an ethical code of life.

Modern Society has affected man in two ways at the same time, he has become independent, self-reliant, critical and ego-centric on the one hand and isolated, alone, afraid on the other. The two processes have gone through together and are two aspects of a dynamic system viz. the individual. It is sometimes difficult to see both these aspects, especially the inner processes. We are prone to imagine that the problem of freedom lies in gaining more and more freedom from external restraints: social, political and moral. This is the traditional freedom which undoubtedly has to be increased and maintained but we have also the more important and difficult task of acquiring and realising our own individual selves and becoming more and more free in our mind in our spirit. This is sometimes known as spiritual freedom. All other types of freedom are but stages towards the ultimate goal.

Democracy has enormous possibilities which have yet to be realised. There may be no retreat but a move forward in the confidence that the enlargement of freedom of the individual in a democracy would make for his full development. All this would need a new orientation of the various socialisation process like family upbringing, education, community organisation, communication system etc. Once the individual is trained and oriented into these other dimensions of his democractic existence, he would find that he has struck new roots and has found new security system for himself. This would mean that democracy is a system of new culture, for it is a whole way of life. The hope of democracy lies in exploiting and elaborating the multi dimensional character of the concept. We have to guard against accepting its two restricted meanings; we have to understand it in a sense such as would permit room for the fullest development and flowering of the possibilities of man.

Gandhiji believed in human freedom and denounced all kinds of suppression. He believed that the ideal society of his conception should be an "ordered anarchy." Such a society would carry the ultimate value of non-violence, freedom, equality and social equilibrium.[2]

Gandhian philosophy viewed in terms of its ideology, ideals, agencies and theories, can help us to find out the evils of our times and provide us some answers to our questions. We shall reinterpret Gandhiji with the postulates ideology, ideals, agencies and a theories in the field of his conceptualisation of individual and the model of a normal society our interest in the field of his individual society relations is qualified by two important points.

1) The controversy of individual versus society as to who influences and dominates whom and, (2) Our own present engagement for carving out and designing a society for our country. Our object here then is to assess Gandhiji in terms of the "individual" and the model of his society.

In terms of ideology, Gandhiji was very much sumpathetic than hostile in the Indian Society. As Professor Saran observes: "His sympathy take the form of approval of the "whole" and criticisms of "parts."[3] This puts him to the liberal school of political opinion.

In Gandhiji, we find a comprehensive concept of freedom. Gandhiji claimed that his conception of freedom signified "the freedom of man in all his majesty."[4] To him freedom is a process of growth inquest of coherent moral purpose and actions.

Gandhiji's devotion to individual rights made him a fighter for democratic freedom. He stressed communal unity and the absolute elimination of untouchability among the foundations of political freedom. Only a community constituted by persons imbued with a sense of deep social cohesiveness can attain the benefit of Swaraj. Hence it is essential to combine the quest for political individuality with the voluntary acceptance of social and political discipline which is the basis of social solidarity and cohesiveness.

According to Gandhiji, moral and spiritual freedom depend on the effective cultivation of the two ancient virtues of truth and non-violence. He never accepted the view of freedom as arbitrariness or licence. Genuine Swaraj is a function of the development of inner sources of power.[5]

Ideally, Gandhiji visualised a stateless society and repudiated the authority of the state at every level and in every form. Gandhiji was convinced that mere constitutional structures will not suffice for the concrete realisation of rights and hence he postulated the ideal of "Rama Rajya" which means the kingdom of love, justice and righteousness. This amounts to the synthesis of the Augustian conception of the kingdom of God on earth with the democratic ideal of the sovereignity of the people. Gandhiji believed in "Sovereignity of the people based on pure moral authority."

Traditional deprivation of the backward sanctions based on ascription was shifted to relative deprivation based on the new values of freedom and equality. Exploitation, suppression illiteracy, poverty and host of other malpractices prevalent in the structure were opposed by Gandhiji. Gandhiji championed the concept of equality on metaphysical grounds. Everyman is equal in the eyes of God as the Bhagavad Gita points out. Hence every man should be legally, politically and socially equal. This presupposes his faith in justice. Gandhiji observes : the first condition of non-violence is justice in every department of life."[6] The chief evils against which Gandhiji fought were racialism, imperialism, communalism and untouchability. His crusade for the liberation of the suppressed lower classes in India shows his deep attachment to the concept of Social and economic justice.[7]

In the social sphere, Gandhiji upholds the "Varnasramadharma" though not the caste system as it exists today. Gandhiji lays stress on functions being hereditary, because heredity is a law of nature. But he is against rigid divisions. Thus Varna according to Gandhiji is intimately, but not indissolubly, connected with birth. He explains why Varna restricts man, for the purpose of holding body and soul together.

Varnasramadharma defines man's mission on earth. He is not born day afterday to explore avenues for amassing riches and to explore different means of livelihood; on the contrary, man is born in order that he may utilise every atom of his energy for the purpose of knowing his maker. It restricts him therefore, to the occupation of his forefathers. That and nothing more or nothingless is Varnasramadharma. Gandhiji pleaded for restoration of the essential principle on which the original Varna was based — the elimination of competition and the realisation of common good through duties to proportion to one's attainments and faculties. In Varnasrama, there was and, there should be no exploitation of intermarriage or interdining.

The unique nature of the Hindu World View with its idea of unity at one level and relativism-pluralism on another finds full expression in all sphere of human activity, thought, philosophy etc. The Hindu believe that the essence of Hindu religion—Sanatana dharma is the essence of life and it would survive against the ravages of time and other influences.

In this context, let us analyse the concept of social equality. This involves the right of each individual to follow the kind of life he desires, take up the occupation he desires, eat, marry and associate with whom he likes, in so far as his actions do not contradict the same right of others. This idea further requires that the same sort of transgression of laws. Similarly, economic equality as to buttress social equality. As at present only equality within a society is possible, universal human equality requires a world society without national barriers which appears to a distant goal. However, metaphysical and social equality of all men can be engendered if all become convinced that the origin and goal of all human beings and their nature are the same. This may in due course of time pave the way towards the establishment of social justice and economic equality.

Gandhiji's inestimable contribution to political theory extends beyond social and political methodology into the realms of political thought. There it challenges the basic assumptions of the main steam of political theory which has assumed a separation of means and ends. The significance of Satyagraha here is that it points to the necessity of bringing means and ends together through a philosophy of action.

Gandhiji believed that on this God's earth—all men are equal, all men are brothers. Gandhiji compares humanity to a huge tree having countless branches and leaves, through all which throbs the same life. The universe is full of endless variety. Men may differ in size, colour and quality, in material possession and property, in talents and dispositions but the soul beneath every human heart is the same for all.

"The recognition and realisation of this essential on evers of the human soul inevitably leads to the belief in the equality of man. Gandhiji declares his own faith in such equality—"I believe implicitly that all men are born equal. All brethren born in India or in England or America or in any circumstances whatsoever—have the same soul as any other. I consider that it is unmanly for any person to claim superiority over a fellow being. He who claims superiority, at once forfeits the claim to be called a man".[8]

Gandhiji believed it immoral to treat a person inferior in any sense. Gandhiji strongly condemned the evil of untouchability among Hindus. He remarked "If we believe, that we are all children of one and the same God, and that God is Truth and Justice, how can there be any untouchability amongst us, His children? God of Truth and Justice can never create distinctions of high and low among His own children... . Just as in the eyes of parents all their children are absolutely equal so also in God's eyes all his creatures must be equal."[9]

Gandhiji regarded untouchability as a big blot on Hinduism. He says, "To deprive a man of his natural liberty and deny to him the ordinary amenities of life is worse than starving the body. It is the starvation of soul the Dweller of the body."[10] Gandhiji's Doctrine of Trusteeship is nothing but an attempt to minimise the gap between the rich and poor. He believed in the concept of Sambhava preached in Bhagavad Gita. All land belongs to Gopal, where is the question of possessing it. We are all trustee of the wealth, talent opportunity or any asset given to us by the Almighty. We cannot claim to be owner of them.

In his ashrams—principle of equality. was followed by him and his followers. It was a co-operate living with equal opportunity to all. Gandhiji did not believe in the arithmetical equality of things. People are born with different capacity and abilities. Gandhiji believed that everybody should receive according to his need. Gandhiji considered himself a true socialist.

A comprehensive programme of non-violent social change as viewed by Gandhiji has three main parts: (1) Improvement of individuals in their ways of living (2) a constructive programme to begin building a new social order even as the old one still exists, and (3) the practice of various forms of non-violent action against social evils.

The Gandhian programme of rural reconstruction included the following use of Khadi, development of village industries socio-economic equality, communal unity, removal of untouchability prohibition of equal status for women, national language and adoption of basic education.

The Gandhian concept of rural reconstruction implies all the four elements, i.e., a process a method, a programme and a movement but with one significant difference. Gandhiji wanted the people to depend entirely on their own resources without any external help from the government either technical or financial.

The major goals of community development are entirely Gandhian to induce social change for balanced human and national betterment, to strengthen the institutional structure in such a way as to facilitate social change and the process of growth, to ensure the fullest possible popular participation in the development process and to promote social justice by permitting the less privileged groups to give expression to their aspirations and to participate in the development activities. As a pragmatist to the core, Gandhiji gave his constructive programme to solve the conundrums of life. Man is an entity by himself. Only a person of homogeneous existence will be able to help his neighbours to raise to the occasion. Gandhiji's aim in life was "to wipe every tear from every eye". Thus it is seen that a man of clear-cut conviction will be better able to render service to the needy.

Those who believe in the efficacy of Gandhian approaches and ideas will have to enrich the intellectual world is dominated by three sets of major ideological systems; liberalism, capitalism and religious fundamentalism. It is the duty of a Gandhian to provide correct, rational, and ethical alternatives—the seminal elements of which are all there in Gandhi's statements and other works. But these ideas have to be proper by developed so that they can meet new challenges.

The Gandhian approach is far superior to other approaches in that it has no fixed models. For each situation, a unique model has to be constructed. No global movement of international non-violent non-cooperation or co-operation will have a chance or survival if it is not perpetually revisionistic, dynamic and realistic. Commitment to violence cannot guarantee security but universal commitment to practical non-violent alternatives can make us personally, national and globally much more secure.

Freedom to Gandhiji is not a licence to the strong to exploit the resources of the weak, Freedom is the passport to every citizens, the charter that allows him to think out his thoughts, merily and work out his theme without let or hindrance. According to Gandhi, the architect of India's freedom, "A free democratic India will gladly associate hereself with other free nations for mutual defence against aggression and for economic co-operation. She will work for the establishment of real world order based on freedom and democracy, utilising the world's knowledge and resources for the progress and advancement of humanity."[11]

To him "Freedom carried a broad interpretation. It does not mean only political freedom, i.e., transfer of political power. It meant much more. It included freedom of thought and action for every individual. It meant freedom to earn an honest living by true and peaceful means. It means co-operation among all. It meant no exploitation, no bondage. It implied discipline. Gandhi strived for freedom anywhere be it India or abroad. His freedom strife for was applicable not to India along but to entire world. He considered freedom for all living on this earth. Such was his concept of the "freedom". He believed in the principle that "No one is free till everyone is free."[12] Thus freedom is one of the basic necessities of human life. Without it no human welfare can take place. It is the essential condition for human survival. Because "what shall we gain for ourselves or for our community if all of us are slaves in a slave country? And what can we lose if once we remove the shakles from India and breath the air of freedom again? Do we want outsiders who are not of us and who have kept us in when they deny us the very right to freedom."[13] "Liberation cannot be achieved without risk."[14] Therefore, all of us have to strive for it.

Modern man cannot but be aware of the dialectical direction of the telos of his own scientific technological enterprise—an enterprise in which he sees himself pardigmatically. Nor again even amidst the encouragements of staggering advances in knowledge and technological power can he fail to be aware that he is moving in a Satanic direction, since the mystery of the universe can never be finally dissolved—involving as it does the unintelligible notion of knowledge and power of creation—exhihilo.

To establish peace, the following aspects may be considered:

(1) A conviction of the fundamental unity of the human family and the equality and dignity of all human beings.

(2) A sense of sacredness of the individual person and his conscience.

(3) A sense of the value of human community.

(4) A realisation that might is not right, that human power is not self-sufficient and absolute.

(5) A brief that love, compassion, selfishness and the force of inner truthfulness and of the spirit have ultimately greater power than hate, enmity and self-interest.

(6) A sense of obligation to stand on the side of the poor and the oppressed as against the rich and the oppressed.

(7) A profound hope that good will finally prevail.

(8) Man's spiritual and moral maturity must grow proportionately to his technical skill and power. It can be done if science and religion get together and work together in a harmonious relationship.

(9) Commitment to violence cannot guarantee security, but universal commitment to practical non-violent alternatives can make us personally nationally and globally much more secure.

(10) "Education for Peace" must be a subject for bringing forth creative human potential in the family, work, place and community.

(11) No scheme of global peace can prove lasting unless it is linked to the creation of a new equitable world economic order. There can be no lasting world peace unless the basic factors of exploitation and hegemony are removed.

(12) The greatest need today more than ever before is to educate the people and their governments to have a greater understanding and awareness of the problems created by armaments race and of the need for disarmament.

If follows that the problem of peace and security is related to the profound and turbulant changes of our time and hence requires an agenda of structural transformation and cultural change necessitated by this turbulance. We will have to include in the paradigm of peace the need to build human and intellectual capabilities for carrying through major restructuring of human polity, with minimum recourse to violence and human destruction and by arresting the suicidal and self-destructive productivities in human culture and psyche.

Peace in the world is impossible without the great powers of earth renouncing their imperialistic designs. This is possible only when great nations, cease to believe in the destructive competition and desire to multiply wants and increase their material possession. Peace requires simplicity in life, we cannot live in peace if we multiply our wants everyday because it gives way to unhealthy competition among human beings.

Gandhiji observed, "I have been taught from my childhood, and I have tested the truth by experience that primary virtues of mankind are possible of cultivation by the meanest of the human species. It is this undoubted universal possibility that distinguishes the human from rest of God's creation. If every great nation was unconditionally to perform the supreme act of renunciation, many of us would see in our life time visible peace establish on earth."[15]

Gandhiji considered that unconditional renunciation by the powerful nations is the pre-condition for the establishment of peace on earth.[15] Gandhiji derived that peace on earth is essentially attached to the moral conduct of human beings. And moral conducts should be the guideline of our day-to-day life. Thus he observed, "Moral principle have no meaning unless they can be made to serve as guides of conduct in the daily affairs of men."[16]

Peace does not imply any kind of cowardice to him. Peace of weak was not accepted to him. According to Gandhiji a strong willed and able to protect oneself—person can achieve and establish peace. Gandhiji believed that cowardice as worse than violence. "I do believe that, where there is only a choice between cowardice and violence, I would advice violence."[17] At other place Gandhiji opined "I would rather have India resort to arms in order to defend her honour than that she would in a cowardly manner become or remain a helpless witness to her own dishonour."[18]

Thus Gandhiji's appeal for non-violent methods to establish peace never included peace of cowards. Self-prestige, honour was supreme to him. Gandhiji believed that strength did not come from physical capacity. It comes from an indomitable will. We see that Gandhiji's view on "Peace" has gone several changes. At one place Gandhiji talked about a "state of absolute peace"—where there will be no violence between nations. At other occasion Gandhiji himself advocated the maintenance of an international police force for controlling violent outbreaks, between nations, in a non-violent world order.

Gandhiji's Philosophy of freedom awakens both types of men from their ignorant attitudes and direct them to unite together under the umbrella of equality. Thus, it grants ample strength to every individual in the society to condemn all kinds of narrow and blind practices which are carried on, in the name of tradition.

A mad rush for the Western material comforts always and in constant dependence, dissatisfaction, cut- throat competition, exploitation and hatred. This will certainly bind the Indians with the threads of untruth and violence and throws them into the ocean of unfreedom. This is why, Gandhiji, time and again, preached the practice of Swadeshi spirit, which contributes to the self-satisfaction and the complete utilisation of native goods. Thus Gandhian conception of freedom gives warning to all who blindly copy the western materialistic civilisation.

Gandhiji sought to prepare us for life in a disarmed world. We must pull ourselves of the world of strive and hatred and be prepared to work unitedly with a sense of harmony and peace. Peace is not the absence of conflict but the ability to cope with it. It was in this spirit that Gandhiji worked and prayed towards the realisation of peace among men. The Gandhian message posses demands on man for the cultivation of good will, love and non-violence, because man, in Gandhian view, is supposedly capable of responding. Man must revaluate himself, subdue his flesh to his soul, limit his wants, and teach himself self-effort sacrifice and non-violence. On the basis of this transformation the world would know genuine peace that would apply equally well to inter-personal affairs as well as to international ones. While fundamental assumptions cannot be proved or disproved and perfection is impossible, still perfectability is always possible.

Gandhiji has left his footprints on the sand of time. His message is a beacon of light to guide us forward in our universal Quest for Truth and Peace. Gandhiji's whole life was but a Saga of spiritual action. Gandhiji sharpened the weapon of Satyagraha and demonstrated to the world its potency.

May the life and teachings of Mahatma Gandhi be a beacon of hope and courage to all of us. The teachings of the Mahatma will continue to be relevant till humanism, betterment of the human condition, world peace, and conflict of resolution by non-violence continues to be relevant and urgently desirable. Let us catch the spirit of Gandhiji's teaching and help to create the kind of society that the Mahatma envisaged. Gandhiji called upon humanity to strengthen its conscience, steel its will, and be ready for the highest sacrifice for establishing the truth of human equality, dignity, fraternity and freedom.

Gandhiji believed that love shall rule the world. Gandhiji has proved that at least for a time, moral force can defeat machine guns. After realising world's present condition, we have to accept his claim.

Reference:

(1) Eknath Easwarn—*Gandhi The Man*

(2) M.K. Gandhi, *Harijan*, 22-3-1946.

(3) A.K. Saran, *Gandhiji's Theory of Society and Our Times*, Allied Publishers, New Delhi, 1970, P. 49.

(4) M.K. Gandhi, *Harijan*, June 7, 1942.

(5) T.S. Devadoss, *Sarvodaya and the Problem of Political Sovereignty*, University of Madras, Madras, 1974, P. 453.

(6) M.K. Gandhi, *Economic and Industrial Life and Relations*, N.P.H. Ahmedabad, vol. III, P. 123.

(7) T.S. Devadoss, *Hindu Family and Marriage*, University of Madras, Madras, 1979, P. 21.

(8) *Journal of Gandhian Studies*, ed. J.S. Mathur, Institute of Gardhian Thought and Peace Studies, University of Allahabad, April, 1987, P. 100.

(9) *Ibid*—P. 101.

(10) *Ibid*—P. 10.

(11) Asha Devi Arayanayakam—*Gandhi The Teacher.*

(12) Michael Randle—*Peace News*, 30th May 1975.

(13) Jawaharlal Nehru—*India's Freedom.*

(14) *Peace News*—May 1975.

(15) M.K. Gandhi—*Harijan*, 16-5-1936.

(16) M.K. Gandhi—*Non-violence in Peace and War.*

(17) *Ibid*

(18) *Ibid*

❑ ❑ ❑

Chapter—IV

Modern Social Legislation

Fundamental Rights are of great importance of individual freedom, but these fundamental rights are a very minimal set of rights and therefore, human rights, which are derived from the inherent dignity of the human person and cover every aspect of life and not just a small number of preferred freedom against the state, have tremendous significance. For the large number of people in a developing country, who are poor, downtrodden and economically backward, the only solution for making fundamental rights meaningful would be to restructure the social and economic order so that they may be able to realise their economic, social and cultural rights.

According to Harold J. Laski, "Rights are those conditions to social life without which no man seek in general, to be hímself at his best."[1] Regarding Prof.Hob House, "Rights are what we expect from others and others from us and all genuine rights are conditions of social welfare. Thus the rights every one may claim are partly those which are necessary for the fulfilment of the functions that society expects from him. They are conditioned by co-relatives to his social responsibilities."

Legislation is the enactment by laws. Law is the body of rules, enacted or customary, recognised by a community as binding itself. The function of law is to provide, protect and promote a frame work of social regulation within which the individual citizen can pursue his several notions of what makes for his happiness. The laws may be protective, regulative or of compulsive type. According to Oliver Wendell Holmes said : "Legislation of today is to meet the social needs of yesterday."[2]

In ancient periods common people were oppressed by arbitrary Governments. They had no rights or status, taxation was arbitrary and individual liberties were not recognised. People clamoured and obtained, either peacefully or by force, what may be called political rights. But the mass of the people were still not ensured for a full and contented life and the pursuit of happiness. The state was only concerned with Law and Order and did not restrict individual liberty in many other spheres. The unrestricted individualism and uncontrolled profit motive as an incentive to all private endeavour were its main features. The emphasis, however, shifted gradually from political rights to social rights and it also opined that certain weaker sections must be protected by the State.

Active pursuit of public welfare became the accepted canon of modern political and social philosophy. According to Shri.V.V. Sastri, "The modern State has to discharge its duty to all sections of the people and the frame work that has to be maintained has not only to recognise the status and importance of each individual as a citizen or human being; it must go further and guarantee a fair measure of security for all, must protect the weak against the strong and must ensure that the resources at the disposal of society are used, to the best advantage for the benefit of the whole people."[3]

There is no state religion in India. It only means that in matters of religion, it is neutral. It is the ancient doctrine in India that the State protects all religions but interferes with none.

CASE LAW

Vasudev Vs Vamanji (1881), I.L.R. Bombay 1980. The State can have no religion of its own. It should treat all religions are equal in the eyes of Law. The State does not identify with any particular form of religion but gives equal protection to all forms. The State must extend similar treatment, to the church, the mosque and the temple.

In a secular state the State is only concerned with the relations between man and man. It is not concerned with relation of man with God. It is left to the individual's own conscience. Every man should be allowed to go to Heaven in his own way. Worshipping God should be according to the dictates of one's own conscience.

CASE LAW

Downes Vs Bidwell (1901) 182 U.S. 244. Man is not answerable to the State for the "Variety of his religious views."

CASE LAW

U.S. Vs Ballard. (1944) 822 U.S. 78.

Fundamental Rights are guaranteed by the Indian constitution. According to Supreme Court in the case of I.C. GolakNath Vs State of Punjab AIR 1967 S.C. 1643; has dealt with in details about the nature and function of Fundamental Rights as provided in the Indian Constitution. Fundamental rights are embodied in Part III of the Constitution and they may be classified as follows:

(1) Right to equality (i.e., Articles 14 to 18)

(2) Right to Freedom (i.e., Articles 19 to 22)

(3) Right against exploitation (i.e., Articles 23 and 24)

(4) Right to freedom of religion (i.e., Articles 25 and 28).

(5) Cultural and Educational Rights (i.e., Articles 29 and 30).

(6) Right to Constitutional remedies (Articles 32 to 35).

They are the rights of the people preserved by our Constitution. "Fundamental Rights is the modern name for what have been traditionally known as "Natural Rights."

"Equality before the Law" as held by the Nagpur High Court in Shiva Shanker Vs M.P. State Government. A.I.R. 1951, Nagpur - 58 is negative concept. It means the absence of any special privilege in favour of any individual. Equal protection of the laws as held in the said case is a positive concept which implies equality of treatment in equal circumstances. There is no such thing as absolute equality among men but among equals, the Law should be equal and administered equally, in other words the like should be treated alike. There should not be any special privilege by reason of birth or creed etc. Equality before the Law does not mean that things which are different shall be treated as though they were the same. The Bombay High court has held in Raja Kulkarni Vs State A.I.R. 1951 Bombay 105: Cr. L.J. 1940, that equal protection means that there shall not be arbitrary discrimination in the laws themselves in their administration.

The State has to protect labour from exploitation, women from masculine domination, children from parental indifference and the poor from the dispensation of puritive relief. It has to guard against disease, disorder and immortality and has to deal with those whose behaviour constitutes a threat to general welfare. The State has to provide certain tax-supported services which are directed to the alleviation of distress, prevention of disablement and the rehabilitation of the disabled, and the self-maintenance of the individual.

Social Legislation is that which serves the present social and economic objectives of the nation and deals adequately with current social problems. He term Social Legislation is very comprehensive and may include Legislation affecting social customs like infanticide, sati, sacrifices and child marriage etc., Legislation for the welfare of labour, legislation for the promotion of thrift and self-help through co-operative endeavour, provision of loans to agriculturists on easy terms, relief of indebtedness, by a compulsory scaling down of debts, zamindari abolition, consolidation of holdings, fixing ceiling on land, progressive taxation, town planning, slum clearance, famine relief, measures for public health and education, control of epidemic diseases, control of price competition, prohibition of beggary etc. But here we have to give a specific meaning and a specific content for the term Social Legislation the present context. "The Social Legislation has to concern itself with the promotion of the welfare of individuals and groups. Legislation should be so designed as to invest the life of everyone with a purpose and with the means and opportunities for the fulfillment of the hopes and aspirations of the average citizens in the light of our constitution."[4] The State has to promote the welfare of all (Sarvodaya) but with a declared bias in favour of the needy, neglected and weaker sections of the people.

The Constitution which declares India to be a Sovereign Democratic Republic rests on four basic principles enunciated in its preamble and they read as follows:

"We, The People of India, having solemnly resolved to constitute India into a Sovereign, Socialist, Secular, Democratic, Republic and to secure to all its citizens :

"Justice, Social Economic and Political; Liberty of thought, Expression, Belief, Faith and Worship; Equality of Status and of opportunity; and promote among them all. FRATERNITY assuring the dignity of the individual and the unity and the Integrity of the Nation."[5]

In our Constituent Assembly this twenty sixth day of November, 1949 do hereday, adopt, enact and give to ourselves this Constitution."[5]

In Part III of the Constitution certain fundamental rights have been conferred on the citizens and others living in the country:

a) Under Article 14, Equality before the law or equal protection of the laws is guaranteed to all. Similarly, discrimination against any citizen on grounds only of religion, race, caste, sex or place of birth is forbidden.

b) Article 15 says (1) "State shall not discriminate against any citizen on ground only of religion, race, caste, sex, place of birth or any of them"; (2) No citizen shall, on grounds only of religion, race, caste, sex, place of birth or any of them, be subject to any disability, liability, restriction or condition with regard to (a) access to shops, public restaurants, hotels and places of public entertainment; or (b) the use of wells, tanks, bathing ghats, roads and places of public resort maintained wholly or partly out of State funds or dedicated to the use of the general public.(3) Nothing in this Article shall prevent the State from making any special provision for women and children. (4) Nothing in this Article shall prevent the State from making any special provision for the advancement of any socially and educationally backward classes of citizens or the scheduled caste and the scheduled tribes. Untouchability is abolished and its practice in any form is forbidden (Article 7).

The liberty of the people is guaranteed by provisions that no person shall be convicted of any offence except for violation of all law in force at the time of the commission of the act charged as an offence. Similarly, no person can be detained in custody without being informed of the ground of his arrest and he shall be produced before a Magistrate within a period of twenty four hours of his arrest. Traffic in human beings and beggar and other similar forms of forced labour are prohibited.

The Constitution of India has guaranteed certain Fundamental Rights to the citizens of India and enunciated certain Directive Principles of State policy, in particular, that the state shall strive to promote the welfare of the people by securing and protecting as effectively as it may a social order in which justice, social, economic and political, shall inform all the institutions of the national life and shall direct its policy towards securing, among other things;

(a) that the citizens, men and women equally, have the right to an adequate means of livelihood;

(b) that the ownership and control of the material resources of the community are so distributed as best to subserve the common good;

(c) that the operation of economic system does not result in the concentration of wealth and means of production to the common detriment.

Having regard to these rights and in furtherance of these

principles as well as of declared objective of the Government to promote a rapid rise in the standard of living of the people by efficient exploitation of the resources of the country, increasing production, and offering opportunities to all for employment in the service of the community, the Planning Commission will make an assessment of the material, capital and human resources of the country... formulate a plan for the most effective and balanced utilisation of the country's resources.[6]

The Planning Commission in the First Five Year Plan enunciating the objectives of planning in India points out: "The central objective of planning in India at the present stage is to initiate a process of development which will raise living standards and open out to the people new opportunities for a richer and more varied life."[7] The Planning Commission further points out : "The urge to economic and social change under present conditions comes from the fact of poverty and inequalities in income, wealth and opportunity. The elimination of poverty cannot, obviously, be achieved merely by redistributing existing wealth. Nor can a programme aiming only at raising production remove existing inequalities. The two have to be considered together; only a simultaneous advance along both these lines can create the conditions in which the community can put forth its best efforts for promoting development. The problem, therefore, is not one of merely rechannelling economic activity within the existing socio-economic frame work; that framework has itself to be remoulded so as to enable it to accommodate progressively those fundamental urges which express themselves in the demand for right to work; the right to adequate income, the right to education and to measure of insurance against old age, sickness and other disabilities... . It is in this larger perspective that the task of planning has to be envisaged."[8]

The social legislation passed before Independence may be dealt with under two heads, central and state legislation. Social legislation of the earliest period was only concerned with checking certain evil socio-religious customs. Under the Act of 1829 Sati was prohibited first in Bengal, and then in Madras and Bombay in the following year.

Next in order was the Indian Slavery Act 1843, which prohibited the sale of any person on the ground that he was a slave. The Indian Penal Code followed it up by enacting that the buying and selling of any person as a slave and habitually dealing in slaves is an offence and prescribed severe penalties for it.

Next was the Caste Disabilities Removal Act, 1850, under which it was provided that no person shall be deprived of any right or property by reason of his renouncing or being excluded from the communion of religion or deprivation of caste.

Next in succession were passed the Hindu Widow Remarriage Act, 1856, the Female Infanticide Prevention Act of 1870 and the Special Marriage Act, 1872, which was later amended in 1932. Persons marrying under this Special Marriage Act were given protection from forfeiture of the rights of succession by extending to them the caste Disabilities Removal Act. During the 20th century were passed the Child Marriage Restraint Act, 1929, the Hindu Gains of Learning Act 1930, The Hindu Women's Right to property Act, 1937, the Hindu married Women's Separate Maintenance Act 1946 and the Hindu Marriage Disabilities Removal Act 1946.

Under the Child Marriage Restraint Act the age of marriage for boys was fixed at 21 and for girls at 18 years. The Hindu Gains of Learning Act rendered all gains acquired by any member of an undivided Hindu family by his own earning, the exclusive and separate property of the acquirer. Under the Hindu Women's Right to Property Act, the widow was given a share equal to that of a son in the property of the husband but she could use it only in her life and could not sell or transfer it. The Hindu Married Women's separate Maintenance Act enabled a married woman to claim separate residence and maintenance from her on certain grounds. The Hindu Marriage Disabilities Removal Act validated all marriages between persons belonging to the same Gotra or Pravara or between those belonging to different sub-divisions of the same caste.

The welfare of children, youth and women workers certain Acts were also passed. Among these the important acts for children are, the Apprentices Act of 1850, the Guardian and Ward Act, 1890, the Reformatory Schools Act, 1897, the children pledging of Labour Act, 1933, and the Employment of Children Act 1938. The Factories Act, the Mines Act, the Merchant shipping Act and the Plantation Labour Act also deal with the question of employment of children. They prohibit employment under a prescribed age and also regulate their hours of work.

To protect young girls from exploitation, there are certain provisions in the Indian Penal Code. Example: selling, letting for hire or otherwise disposing of or buying, hiring or otherwise obtaining possession of any girl under 18 years of age for any unlawful or immoral purpose was made an offence. There are also certain provisions in the Indian Penal Code to protect the modesty and to protect women against forced illicit intercourse. There are special provisions in the labour laws for women with regard to hours of work and for health, safety and welfare. Similarly, various acts were passed for the welfare of labour, regulating their condition of employment resolution of disputes, promoting the economic welfare and social insurance such as the Factories Act, 1933, the Workmen's Compensation Act, 1923, the Coal Mines Labour Welfare Fund Act, 1947, the Mica Mines Labour Welfare Fund Act, 1946 etc.

The Provinces of British India (now States) exercised legislation powers over certain fields and under those powers they have enacted certain laws upon matters which fall under their jurisdiction. Example: under the Municipalities Act several provisions deal with matters relating to health, safety and morals. Thus municipal committees have powers to control and licence all places of public entertainment and amusement to prevent begging and solicitation in public places to prevent public gambling and to control brothels. Various provinces had passed children Acts to provide a mode of trial for juvenile delinquents and Borstal Acts to establish Borstal schools. Sometimes special acts were passed for the suppression of immoral traffic, acts against juvenile smoking, prevention of begging and establishment of special homes for beggars. Probation acts for first offenders, acts against prohibition, etc., were passed by the State. So far we have discussed social legislation before Independence. Next, we will discuss social legislation after Independence.

After Independence, there has been good progress in the enactment of social legislation.

(a) Child Welfare

In the field of child welfare, Children Acts were passed by various states before Independence. For example, the Madras Children Act, 1920, Bengal Children Act 1922, Bombay children Act 1924 etc. Under the Criminal Procedure Code, the children could be set to reformatory schools or sent on probation. There were also probation of offenders Acts passed by the states thought they are not confined to children only. The Government of India formulated a bill after Independence to have a uniform and comprehensive children Act, but this could not be passed. A children's Act was passed in the year 1960 which was applicable to union territories also.

(b) Youth Welfare

The suppression of Immoral Traffic Acts were in force in various states before Independence which made provision for rescuing minor girls from brothels and from moral danger. There are also special Acts to prevent minor girls from exploitation such as U.P. Naik Girls Protection Act, 1929, Bombay Devadasi Protection Act, 1934 and Madras Devadasi Act, 1947. There were also Borstal School Acts in various states to accord special treatment to adolescent offenders. The first was the Madras Borstal Schools Act, 1926.

(c) Prison Reform

The first Prisons Act was passed by the Central Government in 1894, which restricted and regulated the use of whipping, cellular confinement and penal diet. It provided for the classification of different types of offenders and tried to secure uniformity of treatment of all offenders and tried to secure uniformity of treatment of all offenders in Jail. After 1919, the jails became a state subject and the State governments tried to provide many amenities to the prisoners under the rules framed by them in consonance with the Prisons Act, 1984. Some novel experiments such as the open prisoners' Camps have also been made to rehabilitate prisoners in a true sense.

(d) Women Welfare

Under the Constitution, women's equality was proclaimed, but out personal laws which were in operation, subjected them to several disabilities. Thus to maintain the dignity of the individual, equality of sexes and establishment of social justice required many changes.

Proposals for reforming the Hindu personal law particularly relating to property has been before the country in one form or the other since forties and the setting up of Rau's Committee to enquire into and suggest reforms in Hindu law itself owes its origin to a private member's Bill in the Central legislature of those day's conferring some property rights on Hindu Females. The Committee while suggesting amendments in the existing law, recommended that the best cause would be to codify the entire Hindu law in successive stages. The Hindu code by Rau's committee was the result of that recommendation.

The Select Committee of Provisional Parliament in 1948 suggested substantial changes. The Hindu Code Bill introduced in the Parliament was in part rigorous attempt to incorporate radical reforms.

In pursuance of its accepted policy to codify Hindu law in gradual stages, the legislature passed the Hindu Marriage Act, 1955 and the second of such positive measure is the enactment of the Hindu Succession Act, 1956 which become law on 17th June, 1956.

The object of Hindu Succession Act, 1956 is to evolve a fairly uniform system of law for all Hindu with respect to interstate succession; remove inequalities between men and women with respect to rights in property and to evolve a list of heirs entitled to succeed on intestacy based on love and affection rather than on religious efficacy.

Thus the main objects may be enumerated as follows:

(1) To evolve a fairly uniform system of law for all Hindus with respect to intestate succession, that is to say, succession to property in respect of which a deceased person has not made a will;

(2) To give a right of inheritance to daughters which previously under all system of pure Hindu law was not given to the daughters.

(3) To evolve a list of heirs entitled to succeed on intestacy based on love and affection rather than on religious efficacy;

(4) The law should be administered as it is found on the statute book and the customs ought not to endeavour to ascertain what this or that gentleman, no matter how eminent he may be, intended to be the statute of law.

According to Law before 1986, Section 125 of Cr. P.C. was in force regarding the maintenance of Muslim Women, equally with the Hindu Woman. Section 125 provides that the Husband is bound to provide maintenance to his wife, children (legal or illegal) and old aged parents. Until 1986 the situation continued. The Courts in India were giving the judgements awarding the maintenance to Muslim wifes also.

Example: Shah Bano's case 1986.

In this case, the court granted the maintenance to the wide even after the divorce, so long she has not remarried. This case caused a sensational agitation among the Muslim community throughout the country. The Supreme Court confirmed the lower court's decision which granted the maintenance to Shah Bano, aged 54 years. The entire Muslim community felt that by the Supreme Court's decision in Shah Bone's case. Section 125 Cr. P.C. overrides the Muslim Personal Law. Thus a great controversy arose. To satisfy the Muslim, our late Prime Minister Rajiv Gandhi made an Act "Muslim Women (Protection of rights on Divorce) Act, 1986."

As per the law after the Act of 1986 changed the previous situation. Now the muslim wife is not entitled to claim maintenance under 125 P.C. Section 5 of the Act of 1986 provides that if both the wife and husband give their consent admitting the Section 125 of Cr. P.C. through an affidavit, then the concerned Magistrate/ Judge shall dispose of the case according to the provisions of the Section 125 Cr. P.C. generally, no husband gives his consent for the trial under Section 125 Cr. P.C. which burdens more liability upon him. While his personal law permits him to pay the maintenance only for a period of Iddat (a small period). Why should he take unnecessary risk and liability? As per Justice V.R. Krishna Iyer, suggested that the Section 5 of the Act 1986 shall have to be amended by withdrawing the power given to the husband, and instead of giving such power to the husband, such power shall have to be given to the wife, who is the aggrieved party, then only the Act can be called as "The Muslim Women" (Protection of Rights on Divorce) Act, else it does not give any fruitful rights to her. So, after the Act of 1986, the Muslim husband is not bound to maintain his wife after divorce. He has to pay maintenance for a small period of Iddat only. Thereafter no liability lies upon him.

One Act after another was being enacted by the various legislatures in India to adapt the Hindu Law to the fast changing social conditions. Social reformers thought of a comprehensive Hindu Code dealing with all aspects of Hindu Personal Law. As a result a Hindu Law Committee was set up in the year 1941. In 1944, the committee was asked to prepare a comprehensive Hindu Code Bill. A Hindu Code Bill was submitted by the committee to the Government in 1947. After deliberations it was split up into 4 parts. One of these parts took the form of Hindu Marriage Act 1955. It received the President of India assent on 18th May 1955 on which day it became the law.

According to Hindu Marriage Act of 1955 the main features are as follows:

(1) It provides for a set of uniform rules regarding marriage applicable to all Hindus.

(2) Monogamy has been made mandatory.

(3) Marriage of a widow is permissible.

(4) Minimum age for marriage is prescribed. That is the Act has laid down minimum age for the marriage 21 years for boys and 18 years for girls.

(5) The Act does not prescribe any particular ceremony to be performed for a valid marriage. It only provides that such a marriage can be solemnised in accordance with the customary rites and ceremonies of any of the parties to the marriage.

(6) The Act also provides for the registration of the marriage but it is not absolute and does not effect the marriages not registered.

(7) The Act contains provisions for restitution of conjugal rights of the parties to a marriage.

(8) It contains specific provisions for the remedy of judicial separation and for termination of marriage.

(9) The Act lays down the circumstances when marriage is void and when it is voidable at the option of the affected party to the marriage.

(10) The Act provides specific grounds on which a decree for divorce can be passed by the court in favour of any party to Hindu marriage.

(11) After the amendment in 1976, the Act contains provisions for divorce by mutual consent.

(12) The Act provides for maintenance pendentelite and permanent alimony.

(13) The Act also makes provision for the maintenance and custody of the children during the pendency of the legal proceedings and also after passing of a decree. That is it contains provisions for legitimacy and illegitimate children.

(14) The Act has abolished the difference between Mitakshara and Dayabhaga Schools in connection with the prohibited

degrees of relationship for the purposes of Hindu marriages.

(15) The Court can pass orders regarding the custody, maintenance and education of the minor children, if any of the parties in any proceeding under the Act.

(16) Marriage between persons belonging to Hindu, Jaina or Sikh religion is valid under the Act.

Under the Hindu Marriage Act, 1955 certain conditions are necessary for a valid Hindu Marriage. Those conditions have been laid down in Section 5 of the Act.

The conditions are as follows:

A marriage may be solemnised between any two Hindus, if the following conditions are fulfilled namely:

1. Neither party has a spouse living at time of the marriage.
2. At the time of the marriage, neither party :
   - (a) is incapable of giving a valid consent to it in consequence of unsoundness of mind, or
   - (b) though capable of giving a valid consent has been suffering from mental disorder of such an extent as to be unfit for marriage and the procreation of children;

     or
   - (c) has been subject to recurrent attacks if insanity or epilepsy.
3. The bridegroom has completed the age of 21 years and the bride the age of 18 years at the time of the marriage.
4. The parties are not within the degrees of prohibited relationship, unless the custom or usage governing each of them permits of a marriage between the two;
5. The parties are not sapindas of each other, unless the custom or usage governing each of them, permits of a marriage between the two.

Section 5 of the Hindu Marriage Act 1955 introduces the rule of monogamy. It enacts that neither party must have a spouse living at the time of marriage. The expression "Spouse" here used means a lawfully married husband or wife. Before a valid marriage can be solemnised both parties to such marriage must be either single divorced or a widow or a widower and then only they are competent to enter into a valid marriage. If at the time of the performance of the marriage rites or ceremonies, one or other of the parties had a spouse living and the earlier marriage had not already been set aside, the later marriage is no marriage at all. Eg., Prakashchander Vs Parameswari (1987 Punj H. 37).

Thus this provision prohibits bigamy. The bigamousmarriage is non-existent. Section 17 the Act lays down that "anymarriage between two Hindu solemnised after the commencement of this Act is void if at the date of such marriage either party had a husband or wife living; and the provisions of Sections 494 and 495 of the Indian Penal Code shall apply accordingly. Under section 494 of Indian penal code it is an offence punshable with imprisonment for a term which may extent to 7 yers and shall also be liable to fine. Under Section 495 of Indian Penal Code if the fact of the early marriage was concealed fromthe spouse it is punishable with imprisonment for a term which may extend to 10 years and shall also be liable to fine. Hene a bigamous marriage is null and void and is made punishale.

One of the most important features of the Hindu succession Act 1956 is that the right of a Hindu female to inherit the property has been duly recognised and she has been madeentitled to take a share equal to the male heirs. Women's estate ha been abolished and whatever property shall be inherited by a Hndu female that shall be her absolute property. The Hindu sucession Act 1956 has abolished impartible estate, not created bystatute. The Act does not apply to the property of a person towhose marriage, provisions of the Special Marriage Act, 1954, pply.

The traditional Hindu law laid down detaild rules regarding minors and guardians. The age of majority unde Hindu Law was 15 years in Eastern and Southern India and 16 yars in other parts of the country. The father was regarded as the first natural guardian of the person and of separate property of his minor children of either sex. Next to him the same position was assigned by the law to the mother. The traditional law relating to minority and guardianship remained in force in the British India and in the Princely states till about the middle of the 19th century. It has wholly been repealed and replaced by the provisions of the legislative enactments including the Hindu Minority and Guardianship Act, 1956. The Hindu Minority and Guardianship Act, came into force on 25th August 1956. In Sections 1 to 13 the Act laid down rules relating to guardianship of Hindu Minors. The Act did not lay down a comprehensive law. In its preamble it is given that it was amending and codifying only certain parts of the Hindu law relating to Minority and Guardianship among Hindus. The Hindu Minority and Guardianship Act 1956, is applicable to all places within the Union of India except the State of Jammu and Kashmir.

Under the Muslim law the age of puberty and the age of majority are the same. The age of puberty was considered as 12 in the case of a boy and 9 in the case of a girl. However, the age of puberty has been held to be 15 in many cases. So normally in the Muslim law a boy or girl who has not attained the age of puberty, i.e., 15 years is considered to be a minor.

Under the Indian Majority Act of 1875 the age of majority is fixed as 18 years. The Act has superseded the provisions of Muslim law in this respect. The act is not applicable to the capacity of any person to act in the following matters, i.e., marriage, dowry, divorce and adoption. In case where a court guardian is appointed either for the person or property of a minor, the minority will extend to the age of 21 years.

According to the provisions of Section 2 of the Shariat Act, 1937, the law of guardianship in cases where the parties are Muslims, shall be the Muslim personal law.

Guardian is a person having the care of the person of a minor or his or her property or of both. Such Guardian includes:

(1) A Natural Guardian

(2) A Guardian appointed by the will of the minor's father or mother.

3) A Guardian appointed or declared by the Court.

4) A person empowered to act as such by or under any enactment relating to any courts of wards.

As per Minority and Guardianship Act 1956, a natural guardian or testamentary guardian had the power to make an alienation of an immovable property in case of necessity or for the benefit of the estate, but not he cannot do so without the permission of the Court. Under the new Act, the custody of a minor child below 5 years shall ordinarily be with the mother, where as under the old Hindu law the father was entitle to the custody of even such a child.[9]

A male Hindu had the right to adopt a son provided he had no son, grandson or great grandson. A wife could adopt a son to her husband but she could not do so during her husband's life time without his express consent.

After her husband's death, she could adopt, but the adoption had to be make to her husband. A daughter could not be adopted by a male or a female Hindu.

The Hindu Adoption and Maintenance Act, 1956, provides for the adoption of boys as well as girls. A widow can now adopt a son or daughter in her own name. A female Hindu who is unmarried or a widow or a divorcee, can adopt a son or a daughter to herself, provided she has not a son, grand son or great-grand son at the time of adoption. The husband can adopt only with the consent of his wife, if she is alive and is of wound mind.

Under the Hindu Adoption and Maintenance Act unchastity of a widow is no ground for refusing her maintenance, though she would forfeit her such right on remarriage as before. Under the Act both son and daughter are bound to maintain the aged or infirm parents, while previously only son was bound to do so.

In the Indian Penal Code to protect the modest and to protect women against illicit sexual intercourse and buying and selling of girls under 18 years, special legislation was passed by the States to check immoral traffic in women. Such Act were the Bombay prevention of prostitution Act of 1923, Madras Act, 1930 etc. However, the most comprehensive Act to control prostitution was passed after Independence in 1956 by the Government of India. The Suppression of Immoral Traffic in women and girls Act, 1956, though does not make individual prostitution as illegal, it gives wider powers to the states to deal with the problem in a systematic manner.

The main function of legislation is to provide protection and promote a frame work of social regulation within which the individual citizen can pursue his several notions of what makes for his happiness. This, however, has to be consistent with the good of the community as a whole.

Reference:

(1) M. Krishnan Nair and A. Gopinadhan Pillai—*Constitutional Law*, 1996, P. 13.

(2) Quoted in *Social Legislation : Its Role in Social Welfare* 1956, P. 1.

(3) Sastri V.V., "*Social Legislation in India*" in Social Welfare in India, 1955, P. 586.

(4) Sastri V.V., *Op. Cit. P.* 588.

(5) *The Constitution of India* (1958), Government of India, P. 1.

(6) *First Five-Year Plan* (1952), P. 1.

(7) *First Five-Year Plan* (1952), P. 7.

(8) *Ibid*

(9) Chadha, P.N., *Hindu Law* (1959), P. 13.

❑ ❑ ❑

Chapter—V

Gandhian Approach to Communal Harmony

In this chapter an attempt is made to analyse the relevance of Mahatma Gandhi's approach to communal harmony. In a vast country like India inhabited by people following a variety of religions, speaking various languages and observing different cultures, customs and traditions, communal harmony is absolutely necessary for national integration, peace and prosperity. Besides, the issue of communal harmony is quite relevant and significant under the present circumstances in which communal frenzy and religious intolerance have been posing a serious threat and danger to our national unity. Before independence, we used to curse the British for communal divide and violence. But foreign rulers are no more here to sow the seeds of communal disruption, division and hatred. An observer's comments, in this connection, are quite relevant and eye-opener:

"It is unfortunate that even after almost five and half decades of independence we need more conciliation committees and more tightening of the official machinery of administration, like our erstwhile alien rulers, than tracing the root of the problem and finding solution to it."[1]

Similar views have been expressed, by an eminent journalist who says that as India approached the 50th anniversary of its freedom, the evil of communalism clouds its horizon as menancingly as it did in that fateful summer in 1947.[2]

Mahatma Gandhi preached non-violence throughout his life and lived and died for communal harmony and unity. He was such a great man who never felt, thought and acted in terms of communalism or narrow sectarianism. He fought for the safeguard of the rights and interests of the minorities. He had no malice, ill-will and animosity towards any community. His soul was an ancient violin wonderfully tuned and radiating focus of goodwill and love. Undoubtedly, centuries together would not dim the image and the splendour of his idealism since his mission in his life was the service of mankind and humanity through love-truth and non-violence (Ahimsa).

Accordingly, when we talk about communal harmony, we cannot forget the contribution of this great man of India. Remember, he was the most unhappy man, upset and very much hurt with the violence and communal hatred all around him. It is a fact that his soul was restless until the last moment of his life and he wished that rather than he be a helpless to communal (Hindu-Muslim) atrocities, he should be removed from this earth. For instance, he openly threw himself into the flames of communal frenzy and communal rivalry in Bengal, Bihar and Delhi. He went on foot from place to place, village to village spending the message of non-violence, love and friendship, brotherhood and mankind, instilling a sense of courage and a ray of hope in the hearts of those cowed down by violence and communal fanaticism. He fully believed and was convinced that communal fanaticism could be eliminated from the ignorant people only through love and compassion, non-violence and service of men irrespective of their caste, colour and creed. Moreover, he had already experienced and realised this essential truth at an early stage when he was in South Africa and held fast to it till his death. Similarly, during the days of the "Khilafat Movement" and the agitation against the "Punjab Wrongs", he laid utmost emphasis of Hindu-Muslim Unity by which expression he meant communal harmony and unity in its widest sense. His writings and speeches delivered on different occasions in those days are full of passionate appeal for strengthening communal harmony and amity which were then manifesting themselves and for making them a permanent feature of our national life. It was on account of his strong desire to establish harmony between the Hindus and Muslims that he went for an all-out effort to help "Khilafat Movement" which he regarded as a movement for the redress of a very genuine grievance of the Muslims and he hoped that by rendering them assistance during that period of their trial the Hindus would be winning their lasting good will. His policy as well as intention always was to ask the Hindus to leave it to the Muslims not to do anything which could hurt their religious feelings and to ask the Hindus to see to it that nothing was done by them which could hurt the Muslims. For instance, one major cause of conflict between the Hindus and the Muslims, particularly in Northern India, used to be the slaughter of cows especially on the day of Bak-rid. Gandhi in the days of "Khilafat Movement" used to say that it was for the Muslims to protect the cow and it so happened that in 1921, when the Non-cooperation Movement was at its height, cow sacrifice on the day of Bak-rid was almost negligible in the country as a whole. Speaking on the vow of Hindu-Muslim Unity, Gandhi advised that meetings should be seriously considered. He expressed that before the unity became a reality, both the communities would have to give up a good deal and would have to make radical changes in their ideas. He pointed out: "Members of one community when talking about those of the other at times indulge in terms so vulgar that accentuate the relations between the two. In Hindu society we do not hesitate to indulge in unbecoming languages when talking of the Mohammedans and vice versa."[3] Similarly, he pointed out that the standing complaint of Hindus against Muslims was the latter were beef-eaters and that they purposely sacrificed cows on the Bak-rid day. Now it was impossible to unite Hindus and Muslims so long as Hindus did not hesitate to kill their Muslim brothers in order to protect the cow. He explained: "For I think it is futile to expect that our violence will ever compel Mohammedans to refrain from cow-slaughter. I do not believe the efforts of our cow protection societies have availed in the least to lessen the number of cows killed every day. I have had no reason to believe so. I believe myself to be an orthodox Hindu and it is my conviction that no one who scrupulously practices the Hindu religion may kill a cow-killer to protect a cow.

There is one and only one means open to a Hindu to protect a cow and that is that he should offer himself as a sacrifice if he cannot stand its slaughter. Even if a very few enlightened Hindus thus sacrificed themselves I have no doubt that our Musalman brothers would abandon cow-slaughter. But this is Satyagraha, this is equity, even as, if I want my brother to redress a grievance I must do so by taking upon my head a certain amount of sacrifice and not by inflicting injury on him. I may not demand it as of right. My only right against my brother is that I can offer myself as a sacrifice."[4]

Again to him it was only when Hindus were inspired with a feeling of pure love of this type that Hindu-Muslim Unity could be expected and as with the Hindus, so with the Muslims. He said that the leaders among the latter should meet together and consider their sacrifice, when both try to do their duty towards one another instead of pressing their rights, then and only then would the long-standing differences between the two communities could cease. Each must respect the other's religion, must restrain from even secretly thinking ill of the other. We must politely dissuade members of both the communities from indulging in bad language against one another. To him, only a serious endeavour in this direction could remove the estrangement between the two. "Our vow would have value only when masses of Hindus and Muslamans join in the endeavour."[5]. This naturally led to people to hope that the Hindu-Muslim tangle could be solved. Similarly, another cause which used top stir up feelings and led to trouble between the two communities was the question of music accompanying processions in momentum particularly after the advent of the Simon Commission. Late Dr. Rajendra Prasad observed: "The British Government was also interested in encouraging a fissiparous tendency. It ultimately led to the formulation by the Muslim League of its demands which would put the Muslim community in a position of parity as against all the rest of the people although they were less than 25 per cent of the population. The theory that Hindus and Muslims constituted two separate nations was sedulously propagated and when it was accepted by the Muslim League, it led to the demand for a partition of the country and the establishment of Pakistan."[6]

However, it must be mentioned here that though there were some Muslims who were opposed to this yet it cannot be denied that the majority of the Muslims supported this movement whole heartedly and the country had to yield at last. Even during all this period of more than 20 years Gandhi held fast to his views about Hindu-Muslim unity and his opposition to the theory of two Nations.

In spite of this misunderstanding of his actions and motives, he never wavered in his faith. Moreover, like some Muslims, some groups of Hindus also considered his activities as against and prejudicial to the Hindus blaming him for showing undue favour and yielding too much to the Muslim. It was due to the fact that such Hindus never felt that the policy of appeasement which the Mahatma had been following would ever hear fruit. Some of them even did not hesitate to accuse him of treachery to the Hindus. Even after that Gandhi did not bother about his life and felt the agony and rushed to Bengal to stem the tide of communal hatred that had manifested itself in such an ugly shape after the ruthless killings in Calcutta and the atrocities that were committed in Noakhali and other places in East Bengal followed by the terrible happenings in Bihar in 1946. His heart was broken when the disaster followed the partition of the country. History is witness to his tireless efforts made to bring about communal harmony and stem the waves and to heal the wounds. Moreover, it is due to tireless effort and secular attitude of the Mahatma that the exodus of many Muslims from India was stopped and today India has a Muslim population in millions spread all over the country. However, the happening and incidents of that period had so soured his heart that he had almost ceased to have any interest in life. He expressed it publicity time and again that he had no desire to live and be a helpless witness to what had been going on in the country. At the same time he had never lost faith and he was working and hoping for the day when relations of concord and harmony could again be established between the Hindus and Muslims and when those who had migrated to the other side would not only find it possible to return to their old homes but would actually be welcomed by the members of the other community. He was therefore, opposed to anything being done which could make the return of those who had migrated impossible. It shows that his whole policy had been based on an unalterable faith in human nature and a firm belief in non-violence.

Gandhi believed that irrespective of one's religion and faith, one had to feel his identify with everyone of the millions of the inhabitants of our motherland. He said: "In order to realise this every congressman or (anybody else) would have to cultivate personal friendship with persons representing faiths other than his own. He should have the same regard for the other faiths as he has for his own."[7] Similarly, he was not happy while to the disgraceful cry at the railway stations such as "Hindu Water" and Muslim Tea", and separate rooms or pots for Hindus and non-Hindus in schools and colleges, communal schools, colleges and hospitals.[8] In 1938, Gandhi elaborated: "My Hinduism is not sectarian. It includes all that I know to be best in Islam, Christianity, Buddhism and Zoroastrianism. I approach politics as everything else in a religious spirit. Truth is my religion and ahimsa is the only way of its realisation. I have rejected once and for all the doctrine of the sword. The secret stabbings of innocent persons, and the speeches I read in the papers are hardly the thing leading to peace or an honourable settlement"... . I go as a life-long worker in the cause of Hindu-Muslim unity. It has been my passion from early youth. I count some of the noblest of Muslims as my friends. I have a devout daughter of Islam as more than a daughter to me. She lives for that unity and would cheerfully die for it. I had the son of the late Muazzin of the Juma Masjid of Bombay as a staunch inmate of the Ashram. I have not met a nobler man. His morning Azans in the Ashram rings in my ears as I write these lines during midnight."[9]

Similarly, Gandhi emphasised that the Gita, the Koran, the Bible, the Granth Sahib and the Zend Avasta contained gems of wisdom. Now it is up to the followers whether they follow or believe their teachings.[10] In this respect, Gandhi's comments on the subject are quite relevant when a deputation of the Hindus and the Sikhs from Rawalpindi and Dera Gazi Khan met him and explained their grievances to him. Gandhi's reply was that the Hindus and the Sikhs had made Rawalpindi what it was. They were all well off there but became refugees without shelter later on. It hurt him deeply. Why should innocent persons—Hindus or Sikhs or Muslims—be killed in the name of religion? Religious intolerance is one of the major reasons for this problem. Gandhi had admitted that religion was the personal affair of each individual but it must not be mixed up with politics for that matter.[11] And the Hindus, the Muslims, the Sikhs, the Christians, the Parsees, the Jews should be Indians first and Indians last.[12] While elaborating this issue Gandhi remarked: "If some misdirected individual took it into his head to desecrate a temple or break idols, should a Hindu in return desecrate a mosque on that account? Did it anyway help to protect the temple or to save the cause of Hinduism?"[13]

Gandhi pointed out that he was as much as idolworshipper as an idol-breaker, and he believed that all Hindus and Muslims upheld the same view whether they admitted it or not. He said that mankind thirsted for symobolism. He questioned: Were not Masjids or Churches or for the matter Gurudwaras in reality the same as Mandirs (Temples)? He answered that God resided everywhere no less in stock or stone than in a single hair on the body of men. But men associated sacredness with particular places and things more than with others. Such a sentiment was working of respect when it did not mean restrictions on similar freedom for others. To every Hindu and Muslim Gandhi's advice was that if there was compulsion anywhere, they should gently but firmly refuse to submit to it. Personally, he himself would hug an idol and lay down his life to protect it rather that brook any restriction upon his freedom of worship. That required courage of a higher order than was needed in violent resistance.[14] Thus it is on that ground that Gandhi declared time and again that he would not give up repeating the names of Rama and Rahim which meant to him the same God.[15]

Furthermore, in the eventuality of a communal conflict Gandhi's advice is that we should forget the past and learn the duty of having friendly feelings towards all and being inimical to none.[16] He reminded, for example, that the crores of Muslims were not all angels nor were all the Hindus and the Sikhs. There were good and bad specimens among all communities. Would they be less than friendly towards the so-called criminal tribes amongst them?[17] In such circumstances both men and women of one communities and establish friendship with them. Besides they should invite them on ceremonial occasions and be invited. The girls and boys of various communities should be attracted to common rather than communal schools. They should mix in sports. He pointed out: "The condition of keeping me in your midest is that all the communities in India live at peace with one another, not by force of arms but that of love... there is no better cement to be found in the world."[18]

That is why once Gandhi advised the people of India as a whole not to be violent and take the law into their own hands and commit in human acts. To him that would mean the end of society.[19] Therefore, Gandhi realised the importance of self purification which could purge out the dross from the hearts of the conflicting communities. Accordingly, all should turn the searchlight inward and to cast out all hidden impurity. In April 1946. Gandhi stayed in the quarters of an untouchable (Harijan Colony) in Kingsway, Delhi and as usual started conducting a public prayer meeting there every evening. The first evening he asked those present whether they would object to the recitation of some verses from the Koran. Many of them objected to it. They told him that he had no authority to intone or use an Islamic holy book at Hindu service. On that point Gandhi broke off the meeting. He raised the same question the next evening. Again there was opposition to it. Likewise, Gandhi also refused to pray with the congregation. The same thing happened the third evening. Gandhi repeated the same thing fourth evening. As a result and to everyone's surprise, no one objected as the objectors had withdrawn. In the end, non-violence prevailed and Gandhi proved to be victorious.

CONCLUSION

When we come to Gandhi's approach to communal harmony, we find that Gandhi opposed communal virus of return blow for blow which is nothing but perpetuating our mental slavery and tearing up our motherland into bits, namely, Hindustan, Pakistan, Brahmistan, and Achhutistan[20] (land of Untouchables) and now one more such a place—Khalistan. Everybody knows how dear to his heart was the dream of a united India—a peaceful and a prosperous India—an India in which all Indians, irrespective of their religion, language or political affiliation, could live together as one big family in an atmosphere free from communal frenzy, mutual rivalries and prejudices. He sacrificed himself so that a united India might live together. Dr. Rajendra Prasad has rightly said it was the tragedy of the first magnitude that the unscrupulous people who could not reconcile themselves to his approach to communal harmony, conceived the idea of removing his body from the scene of his activity and achieved success in their design. Similarly, Muslims as a body also did not "fully appreciate the value of his good services till his tragic death, but he bore witness to the truth that was in him by smiling laying down his life for it. No man can do more."[21]

Thus, here lies the importance of Gandhian approach to communal harmony. Today, movements are launched with communal violence and quelled with more violence. Bloodshed continues unabated, communal riots erupt on the flimsiest of provocations. This is more important in the sense that we have been unable to overcome or stop violence by violence or forcible methods. Gandhi had opposed and rejected the theory of return-a-blow-for-a-blow or bullet for-a-bullet, which was not the solution of any of our problems. It is the height of communal virus when we have a general rather wrong impression that while a person is being killed in violent incidents in Delhi, we say he would be a Sikh and if another killed in Punjab, he would be a Hindu. Whereas, the truth is that violence does not see a Hindu or a Muslim or Sikh or anybody else. Such a thinking creates undesirable and unethical values such as anger, hatred, suspicion and spirit of revenge. Therefore, there is confusion. Such confusion cannot be removed until and unless we all, irrespective of our caste, colour, and creed cultivate in us higher values and virtues such as liberal attitude, truthfulness, humility, compassion, tolerance and loving kindness which Gandhi preached throughout his life.[22]

Thus Gandhi's approach to communal harmony has a meaning, a worth and is meaningful step in the proper direction but this single step should not be considered as a panacea or a single pill or tablet course for the eradication of a serious disease of communalism. However, this one step of humility, tolerance, liberal attitude, self-restraint, self-purification, love, compassion and loving kindness can show us the proper way to go ahead for the second step to reach our destination – communal harmony, peace and amity. Therefore, the first step is most important, fundamental, and decisive also.

Reference:

(1) B.S. Gupta, "*Education and Integration*" in the Tribune (Chandigarh), 2-11-198, P. 4, Col. 5.

(2) *Ibid*, 1-6-1987, P. 4, Col.5.

(3) *Young India* (Bombay), 7-5-1919, Vol.1, No.1, P. 9.

(4) *Ibid*

(5) *Ibid*

(6) Rajendra Prasad, "*Foreword in M.K. Gandhi, Communal Unity* (Ahmedabad, Navajeevan Publishing House, 1983), Reprinted; P.8.

(7) *Ibid*

(8) *Ibid*

(9) *Harijan* (a journal of Applied Gandhism: 1933-55), (New York, Garland Publishing, INC, 1973), 30-4-1938 Vol. VI, P. 99

(10) *Ibid* 5-10-1947, Vol.XI, No. 36, P. 354.

(11) *Ibid* 7-12-1947, Vol. XI, No. 45, P. 459.

(12) *Ibid*

(13) *Ibid*, 30-3-1947, Vol. XI, No. 45, P.459.

(14) *Ibid*

(15) *Ibid*, 20-4-1947, Vol. XI, No. 12, P. 118.

(16) *Ibid*, 25-1-1948, Vol. XI, No. 52, P. 531.

(17) *Ibid*

(18) *Ibid,* P. 536.

(19) *Ibid,* 1-2-1948, Vol.XII, No.1, P. 10.

(20) *Harijan,* 30-3-1947, Vol.XI, No. 9, P. 86.

(21) Rajendra Prasad, *"Foreword" in M.K. Gandhi Communal Unity, Op. cit.,* P. 7.

(22) *Harijan,* 2-4-1938, Vol. VI, P. 65.

❑ ❑ ❑

Chapter—VI

The Concept of Child Welfare in Gandhi's View

In this chapter an attempt is made to analyse the concept of Child Welfare in Gandhi's view. In the past the state used to be only police state in which the people were expected to obey the commands of their rulers. The welfare of the people was in no way the concern of the rulers. But today the whole concept has changed. Today it is the responsibility of the state to look after the social welfare of the people.

Social Welfare is a very wide term which implies that social advancement of the people should be ensured. The people should be given social justice. Those who are socially backward and downtrodden should be advanced and uplifted. Their rights should be fully well protected and that none should be denied social justice for his being economically poor or downtrodden. All the sections of the society should have adequate living standard and the disparity between the rich and the poor should be abridged to the extent possible. Basic needs of the people i.e., Food, Clothing and Shelter (Roti, Kapada, aur, Makan) should be met as quickly and adequately as possible. It is the responsibility of the state to ensure that all the sections of the society should get their due and nothing is denied to them.

In a Social Welfare State the women are also not denied their due and legitimate rights and considered as equal partners in national constructive and developmental programmes. Similarly the children are properly looked after and it is ensured that they come up as healthy, souńd and strong citizens. Proper medical and schooling facilities are provided to them. Arrangements are made for providing them recreational facilities.

The concept of Child Welfare Services has changed with the changing concept of social work. Helpless and destitute children have been the object of ancient religious charity. But the recognition that all the children are in need of help including the destitutes is a recent phenomenon. In this age the term "Child Welfare" has assumed a broader meaning. It is concerned not only with the case of the maladjusted, and delinquents, but incorporates the social, economic and health activities of public and private agencies, which scare and protect the well-being of all children in their physical, intellectual and emotional development. "Scientific progress in the fields of anthropology, biology, medicine, psychology and social research during the past hundred years has changed the attitude of society towards the child. He no longer is treated as an adult person only smaller in stature but as a human being with his own laws of biological and mental growth. We are aware that the child is following drives, social forces and motivations which are basically different from those which govern adult behaviour."[1]

Child Welfare is important for the child himself, for the family and for the society. It is important for the child himself in the sense that he will be able to perform his duties well, when he has a good physique, a good mind and a good personality. His welfare is good for the family as he forms a part of the family, being its member. His betterment is also the betterment of society, as he is the future loader of the society. The child in this sense is the most important element of society.

According to Milton, he has rightly pointed our "child shown the man, as morning shows the day." The study team on Social Welfare points out: "The importance of Child Welfare Services lies in the consideration that the personality of man is built up in the formative years, and the physical and mental health of the nation is determined largely by the manner in which it is shaped in the early stages."[2] The childhood is the best period for physical, mental and spiritual development. He is the potential force for the nations. He is the future and should be developed on the right lines. He is the present as well as the future. The child is the father of the man. Thus the importance of child welfare hardly needs much emphasis.

CHILD HEALTH

The health of the child is to be guarded at two stages, i.e., at the pre-school stage and at the school stage. Besides, provision has also to be made for the proper nourishment. At the pre-school stage their health is to be looked after along with that of their mothers in the ante-and postnatal stage. This will reduce the rate of infant mortality, which is vary at present as compared to that of other countries, and it will also improve their health.

The number of maternity and child welfare centers before the beginning of the First Five-Year Plan was very small and this was particularly so in the rural areas. Top priority has been given to this programme in the health service under the Five-year Plans.

The Planning Commission in the First Five Year Plan recommended that an adequate number of such centers properly equipped and staffed should be provided in all the Urban Health Organisations. One centre with a minimum staff of one health visitor, two midwives, a peon and a part-time sweeper was to serve a population of 10,000. In addition, there should be a woman doctor preferably in the Post-graduate Training in maternity and child health to be in-chance of these centres. There is over crowding in practically all the maternity hospitals. The number of maternity beds should be increased to double its present strength in order to accommodate more delivery cases and to give post-natal care for a longer period. The post-natal clinics should form an essential feature of all hospitals with maternity beds.

It is also essential to reserve for children at least 10 per cent of the beds where there is no separate children's hospital with adequate number of beds. In the villages the programme is to provide maternity and child health centres as part of primary and secondary health unit centres in each community development block and sub-district area.

Health services for school-going children are very meagre. The corporations and municipalities in cities and towns have been making attempts to conduct annual physical examination of children. But the examination is general cursory and does not give a correct picture of the state of health of the children.

Play is a vital need in the life of the child and his playing activities may be in the home, school or community environments and can take the form of playthings, companionship and play-ground activities. The municipalities in the towns and village panchayats in the rural areas should provide play-space for children. At present the number of such play-grounds equipped with suitable accessories is very small, both in the urban as well as rural areas. This number needs to be considerably increased. Proper maintenance and management of play-grounds are essential. This play-ground service may be provided by voluntary welfare agencies and youth and student organisations.

The extra- curricular activities in schools have opened up a new era in the field of child welfare. But still a large number of our schools are mainly bookish and academic in their programme. Basic education, multi-purpose schools and other extra curricular activities, now started, may go a long way in helping the Indian child develop the power of self-expression and his physical and mental faculties. The Bharat Scouts and guides movements and its affiliated units, the "Balkan-ji-Bari", the "Kishore Dal", "Bachonki Biradari", children's centres and other such movements have been doing a good deal to fill in the leisure hours of the young.

The Programme comprises activities as holiday camps, picnics, outings, tours, educational visits, music, drama and dance festival, special film shows, children's libraries, play parks, sports melas and exhibitions. Among these the "Balkan-ji-Bari" is a developing organisation and its main value lies in bringing together children from all over India in camps and national festivals. The children centres are now being equipped with play-grounds indoor space for a children's library, a dramatic hall, and facilities for developing child arts and handicrafts so that the scope of children's recreations can be extended.

The special scheme of holiday camp was started in 1958 by

the Central Social Welfare Board for children of the age-group ranging from 12 to 16 years and whose parents/guardians were earning Rs. 3000/- or less per annum. It was recognised that well-organised recreational programmes are important for the healthy development of children. The camps were usually organised for 15 days during school vacation or other holidays. The number of holiday camps organised rose from 24 in 1959-60 to 250 in the year 1968-69.

Among the physically handicapped children may be included the blind, the deaf, the dumb and suffering from other physical disabilities. "Like many other countries in the world, India has no system of registering and enumerating handicapped children. Moreover, attention has been given only to a few categories of handicapped children, such as the blind the deaf, the orthopaedically handicapped and the mentally retarded. No statistics regarding other categories of handicapped children are available. Such statistics as are available seem to be based on inadequate sample studies undertaken without scientific definitions. According to the usually accepted estimates, the country has about 0.5 million blind, 0.2 million deaf, 0.5 million orthopaedically handicapped and nearly 2 million mentally retarded children."[3]

The number of separate institutions for the deaf and dumb is very few, and they are mostly looked after along with blind. They are run by voluntary efforts. The state will have to take measures for supplementing their efforts and to start new ones where necessary.

Children suffering from loss of limbs are many. No appreciable efforts have been made to rehabilitate such persons. Orthopaedic departments in various hospitals should supply equipments to such children. There are a large number of children who suffer from T.B. and other physical ailments. There are no special arrangements for the treatment of such children in hospitals. It will be essential to reserve certain beds for such children in these hospitals.

There were only four institutions in the whole of India in the year 1955 which catered to the needs of mentally defective children. The first child guidance clinic was organised in India in the year

1936. The few mental hospitals that are there in the country make no special arrangements for the treatment of the child patients.

The Planning Commission in the First Five Year Plan recommended that at least one child guidance clinic should be brought into existence in every state and where possible such clinics should be organised by municipalities. The organisation of this service is likely to be handicapped for want of psychiatrists. Necessary training will have to be provided in the school of social work to train personnel for them.

The problem of feeble-mindedness did not receive due attention till recently and there was not a single institution in the country to look after and treat the feeble minded children. The psychologists and the educationalists are now gradually giving their attention to this problem and efforts are on foot to start some pilot projects in order to tackle this problem on a comprehensive scale, sufficient number of trained psychologists and psychiatrists will be needed for this purpose.

In an economically underdeveloped country the number of destitute children must be very large. To this may be added the number of children who are virtually destitute in view of the fact that they are without guardians. Such are lone, orphaned, neglected, deserted or destitute children. Children Acts have been passed in various states but they are not very effectively enforced. There are some ashrams, missionary homes, Salvation Army homes, Ramakrishna Mission homes etc. for the destitutes. Besides, there is a large number of unregistered institutions, which very often exploit the needy boys and girls.

The planning Commission in the Fourth Plan rightly observes: "Although Children Acts in most of the states and Union Territories cover both neglected and delinquent for neglected children has not received much attention."[4]

Destitution in general is a part of the poverty at large and child welfare services cannot cope up with it nor can it be expected of them. The solution is to be multi-pronged one. They are as follows:

1. For children whose parents are too poor to afford them

necessary maintenance the latter may be given some allowances instead of sending them to the institutions. The amount should be sufficient to enable the mother to maintain her children suitably in her home, without resorting to such outside employment as will necessitate leaving her children without proper care.

2. For children without effective guardianship, the best method of their rehabilitation is to find a place for them in foster families which system we have yet to develop or in homes of distant relatives with some allowances, if necessary.

3. For those who cannot be cared for in any of the above ways it will be necessary to develop special institutions such as children's villages, boys' towns and similar organisations where a large number of such children could be given protection, shelter, care, education and training, till they are rehabilitated and can function in a normal way.

4. All the voluntary institutions working at present will have to be reorganised to run on scientific lines. All the activities which are necessary for the development of children may be taken with the assistance of trained social workers. They may be assisted by Municipal Committees, Corporations and The State Governments. Those voluntary institutions which are inefficient and small may be amalgamated, where necessary. Many of the agencies are located in unhygienic places and the buildings for keeping inmates are unsuited for healthy living. The problem is mostly of finance and land, which are to be provided by the state Government or Municipal agencies. The programme of these agencies are also not wholesome. In certain orphanages the inmates are asked to collect funds by begging from the public. It will be better if in such cases collections are made by the employees of the institutions.

Child begging is a corollary to destitution. When destitute children are unable to find a place in welfare institutions, they are used as tools for begging. The melodramatic story of a child, tortured, maimed and crippled with a view to making him a better instrument for begging is not unknown. Strict measures will have to be taken in this case. The Third Five Year Plan points out that the children who take to begging are often victims of gangs of exploiters. The Indian penal Code provides for severe punishment of persons found guilty of exploiting children for anti-social purposes and kidnapping or maiming children for the purpose of begging. Children Acts also provide for protection against exploitation of children for anti-social purposes, including begging. Thus the necessary legislation already exists and the main task now is to ensure its effective enforcement."[5]

In juvenile delinquents there are various complexities of the problem of delinquency. At present, only a small number of delinquent children are dealt with and the treatment given to them does not provide for full rehabilitation. The problem of delinquency is extensive because of the prevailing general conditions in which children are brought up. Poverty, neglect, slum life, cruelty or frustration at home or encouragement of delinquent acts by elders, all these factors may lead to delinquency.

In the various states, Children Acts have been passed which deal with delinquent children but there are deficiencies in these Acts:

1. These Acts are not uniform in all states.
2. They are not comprehensive.
3. They are not properly enforced.

Before tackling the problem on a comprehensive basis, the legislation will have to be revised and made uniform. However, the weakest link in the treatment of the problem is the absence of one suitable agency for the enforcement of legislation, the absence of adequate police force, the inadequacy of court facilities, children's institutions and probation officers. The Union Ministry of Education called a conference of public workers in the field of Juvenile delinquency in 1949, which discussed the problem of juveniles thoroughly. To tackle this problem earnestly the planning commission has recommended the following measures:

1. Juvenile aid committees be set up in cities consisting of a small number of selected and specially trained police officials, who will examine cases of delinquents, and deal with cases of minor delinquencies without reference to courts.
2. There is a lesser number of certified schools and fit-person's institutions at present in the country. More institutions will have to be provided for that purpose, with trained personnel.
3. Some Juvenile reformatories exist in some states. They will have to be reorganised to suit the present objective.
4. In no case juvenile delinquents are to be put in correctional institutions where adult under-trials and prisoners live. Besides there is need to have sufficient juvenile courts and remand homes for dealing with juvenile delinquents.

Despite the law's partial prohibition of child employment, children are found employed. The Labour Investigation Committee, which functioned during 1946 and 1947, noted that in various industries and mainly in the smaller ones, the prohibition of child employment is openly disregarded. It has become difficult to enforce the law owing to the inadequacy of the inspection staff. Factory managers are able to obtain fictitious age certificates. Cottage industries and hotels etc., generally employ child labour.

The general improvement of Child Welfare Services in India requires greater co-ordination and better leadership for the innumerable Child Welfare Organisations that exist in this country. The Child Welfare Movement under the guidance of the Indian council for Child Welfare, needs to be encouraged and strengthened. In the new millennium this organisation is to be made more representative of children's organisations in the country.

The Gandhian concept of education is directed towards enabling and helping the child and the youth to develop the personality, physically, intellectually, emotionally and spiritually. Gandhiji says, "True education is that which draws out and stimulates the spiritual, intellectual and physical faculties (power) of the children."[7]

Education is necessary for the child and the youth for a balanced and harmonious development of their personality. In Gandhian view, life is an indivisible unity and cannot be divided into watertight compartments as home life, school life, or as childhood and adulthood.

Gandhian approach to child-and-youth welfare is also based on the recognition of stages of psychological and physical development and of different needs of age groups.

The real education begins from conception, as the mother begins to take up the responsibility of the child. If a mother is correctly instructed and prepared for her coming responsibility then that will be the education of the child as well... .Therefore; pre basic begins with adult education; that is to say, education of parents in wise parenthood."[8] The first stage in child-and-youth welfare envisages the education of the parents for a better parenthood. In Gandhiji opinion, man cannot hope to rule over his self without overcoming lust.

We can conclude that the Gandhian approach to Child-and-Youth Welfare is closely linked with the bigger problems of social reconstruction in the country, and at the same time it is a serious attempt to remake the personality of the child by developing healthy habits and constructive and scientific attitudes on life during the formative period of childhood.

Gandhian approach to the fields of Social Welfare very often envisages basic changes in the social values, social customs and usages and the general frame work of the society. In common parlance, such changes are referred to as social reform. That is why Gandhiji is often called a social reformer.

Gandhhiji accepted the special claim of Children-and-Youths with the realisation that for the establishment of Sarvodaya Social order and sustaining it, the remaking of man was essential. This Gandhiji could do best by looking to the education of the child and the youth. Therefore, Gandhian approach to the field of Child-and-Youth Welfare is a plea for the incorporation of education as a programme of social work.

The Central Children Act, 1960, which provided for the care, protection, maintenance, welfare, training, education and rehabilitation of neglected children was replaced by the Juvenile Justice Act, 1986 to provide uniform pattern of justice to juveniles throughout the country. It came into force from 2nd October, 1987, in all the states except Jammu and Kashmir.

The Child Labour (Prohibition and Regulation) Act was passed in 1986. The main object of the Act is to prohibit the engagement of children (who have not completed fourteenth year of age) in certain employments and to regulate the conditions of work of children in certain other employments.[9] The persons who employ children for begging are now severely dealt with under state prevention. Begging Acts under the Bombay Prevention of Begging Act, 1959, says that any person who uses the child for begging is convicted with punishment up to 3 years. Social legislation is a concerned implementation which requires the co-operation of people.

Reference:

(1) Fried Lander, W.A. *Introduction to Social Welfare* 1955, P. 327.

(2) Study Team on *Social Welfare and Welfare of Backward Classes*, 1959, P. 115.

(3) Report of *the committee for the preparation of programme for children* (1968), P. 47.

(4) G.R. Madan, *Indian Social Problems*, Vol. 2, 1994, P. 106.

(5) G.R. Madan, *Indian Social Problems*, Vol. 2, 1994, P. 107.

(6) *Ibid* P. 107.

(7) *Harijan*, 1-9-1937.

(8) Narulkar, Shanta, *Plan and Practice, Sevagram*, 1938. P. 2.

(9) *Indian Labour Year Book* 1989 (1990) P. 203.

Chapter—VII

The Concept of Women Welfare in Gandhi's View

In this chapter an attempt is made to analyse the concept of Women's Welfare in Gandhi's view. "Women is the mother of the race and it is the liaison between generations. Indian culture attaches much importance to this section of the society; therefore India has been symbolised as Mother India, Keeping in view the exemplary qualities of women, viz, patience, endurance, love, affection, sympathy and generosity. According to Sri. Jawaharlal Nehru, "To awaken the people it is the woman who must be awakened. Once she is on the move the family moves, the village moves, the nation moves." Gadhiji considered "Woman as the incarnation of Ahimsa."

In ancient India the woman were given an equal status along with men almost every field of life. They received higher education and participated in the discussion of political and philosophical nature with male scholars. The Vedas, the Upanishads, the Mahabharat and the Puranas mentioned the names of the lady scholars, Philosophers, poets and politicians in ancient India.

In Mahabharat the wife has been called the better half of the husband. In Aitereya Upanishad, the wide has been called companion of the husband. In Rigveda the wide has been blessed to live as a queen in the house of her husband. The word

"Dampati" so often used in the Vedas characterises both wife and husband. According to Macdonell and Keith this word signifies the high status of women in ancient India.

The medieval period of Indian history which Synchronised with Muslim rule brought further deterioration in her position. The prevailing conditions in the society demanded the protection of woman form the eyes of Muslim rulers and led to the system of "Purdah" which blocked the way of her further progress. Society, having robbed her of individuality, idolised her as "Sati" a tradition of noble sacrifice.

With the advent of British rule a new social era emerged. Western education was responsible for the introduction of a new pattern of thinking whose major characteristics were rationalism, democracy and liberalism. The first social reformer was Raja Ram Mohan Roy who advocated the abolition of Sati" and the act for this purpose was passed in 1829. The other social reformers also championed the cause of women and the result was that certain social reforms were undertaken by them to alleviate the sufferings of women. The problems tackled were remarriage of widows, their education the "Purdah" System the early marriage, their property rights and certain other steps for the welfare of unfortunate women. Some of the important enactments were Hindu Widow's Remarriage Act, 1856, the child marriage Restraint Act, 1929, the Hindu women's Rights to Property Act, 1937. The Welfare institutions included the establishment of Seva Sadans and Widow's Homes to the end of the nineteenth century and onwards.

No man in India has done more than Gandhiji in recent times for the elevation of women and the occupation by them of their rightful place in domestic and public life. A passionate lover of humanity, an implacable foe of injustice in whatever form or sphere, it is small wonder that Gandhiji early espoused the woman's cause. Through out his long life of service Gandhiji preached forcefully against wrongs done to women in the name of law, tradition and even religion. Gandhiji has spoken out fearlessly against enforced widowhood, purdha, the dedication of girls to temples, prostitution, early marriage, dowry system, the economic bondage and material slavery of women.[2]

Gandhiji championed the cause of women. Gandhiji considered woman as the incarnation of ahimsa. Ahimsa means infinite love, which again means infinite capacity for suffering. Who but woman the mother of man, shows this capacity in the large measure ? ... let her forget she ever was or can be the object of man's lust. And she will occupy her proud position by the side of man as his mother, maker and silent leader. It is given to her to teach the art of peace to the warring world thirsting for that nectar.[3]

Gandhiji, in short considered woman as "the personification of self-sacrifice." Gandhiji was against the purdha system. Gandhiji wrote: "chastity is not a hot-house growth. It cannot be superimposed. It cannot be protected by the surrounding wall of the purdha. It must grow from within, and to be worth anything, it must be capable of withstanding every unsought temptation.... The real purdha is of the heart. A woman who peeps through the purdha and contemplates a male on whom her gaze falls, violates the spirit behind it. If a woman observes it in spirit, she is truly carrying out what the great prophet has said."[4]

The root cause of women's degeneration according to Gandhian diagnosis, is to be sought in Hindu culture and age-old religious customs, in man's lust and in the woman herself who has succumbed to the enjoyments. Gandhiji looked to Hindu Culture and religious customs to be the cause of women's lowering of status in the society.

Gandhiji says, "Hindu culture has erred on the side of excessive subordination of the wife to the husband, and has insisted on the complete merging of the wife in the husband. This has resulted in the husband's sometimes usurping and exercising authority that reduces him of the brute."[5] Gandhiji has also pointed out gross violation of the dignity of the woman veiled under custom and tradition. Custom has widely justified making the woman subordinated to man in a wrong sense. Gandhiji says, "By sheer force of various customs even the most ignorant and worthless man have been enjoying a superiority over woman."[6]

As a result of age-long process woman has been degenerated

to her present position. Gandhiji says, "But somehow or other man has dominated woman from ages past, and as women has developed an inferiority complex she has believed in the truth of man's interested teaching that she is inferior to him."[7] Again, "Man has regarded woman as his tool. She has learn to be his tool and in the end found it easy and pleasurable to be such, because when one drags another in his fall, the descent is easy."[8]

Gandhiji, no doubt, blames the religious and cultural customs and the man for the present condition of women but primarily he lays the responsibility on the woman themselves. It is because she has consented to be called the weaker sex; she has considered herself unable to stand on her own without man's protection; she has tacitly acknowledged that she is inferior to man intellectually; she has been flattered by man's tributes to woman's physical beauty and powers of attraction; she decorates herself to please the man and has thereby lowered her own status and standard. Thus she has willingly subscribed to her won subordination, injustice and exploitation. She would have given a lead in the society had she not succumbed to the enjoyments and attraction of her physical; decorations.

Gandhian approach to women's welfare is not so much a protest against a denial of specific rights, example, of property or of occupation or against this or that particular social evil as an underlying resentment against social injustice as such directed towards restoration of women to her natural and rightful place in society as an equal to man. Gandhiji recognises the equal rights of woman with man irrespective of any disability associated with her name. Gandhiji says, "Woman is the companion of man gifted with equal mental capacities. She has the right to participate in the minutest detail of the activities of man and she has the same right of freedom and liberty as he. She is entitled to a supreme place in her own sphere of activity as man is in his. This ought to be the natural condition of things and not a result of learning to read and write."[9]

Gandhi was a harsh critic of women's decorating herself with ornaments. To him, it was a sign of slavery, without the removal of which she could not rise to her heights. Sometimes, women say that they wear ornaments or decorate themselves to please their men and not for themselves. But such a statement itself—deceptive as the women in general have succumbed to the temptation of ornaments, Gandhiji therefore, calls upon the women. "Refuse to be the slaves of your own whims and fancies, and the slaves of men. Refuse to decorate yourselves, do not go in for scents and lavender waters. If you want to give out the proper scent, it must come out of your heart, and then you will captivate not man but humanity. It is your birth right...come to your own and deliver your message again."[10] Thus, Gandhi emphasises that by getting over their own whims and fancies and freeing themselves from the slavery of ornaments they would be able to make spiritual development of their personality.

Gandhiji was never obsessed by the cause of women. But he never pandered to their desires, fancies and whims. Often enough he was as harsh a critic of women's ways as of mans. He was not satisfied with the advance of a few city-lured ladies or sophisticated and educated woman. In fact he deplored certain aspects of their so-called advance. Gandhiji says of the so-called modern girls, "I have a fear that the modern girl loves to be Juliet to half a dozen Romeos. She love adventure.... The modern girl dresses not to protect herself from wind, rain and sun but to attract attention. She improves upon nature by painting herself and looking extraordinary."[11]

Gandhi thus warns the Indian girls that they should not copy the modern western girls as it complicates their problems which have already become a serious menace. For many social evils, as if kidnapping, abduction, eve-teasing, and man's misbeaviour, though men are responsible, yet the problem is further complicated by frailities of the women themselves. Gandhiji therefore, advises them that they should live a simple life and learn the art of protecting themselves against ruffianly behaviour of man.

Gandhiji showed to the women that it was their duty to guard the characters of their husband as they do of their wives and resist whatever evil in them may be. Gandhiji says, "women do not know what influence for good they can exert on their husbands. They wield it unconsciously, no doubt, but that is not enough.

They must have that consciousness and the consciousness will give them the strength, and show them the way to deal with their partners. The pity of it is in their most wives do not interest themselves in their husband's doings. They think they have no right to do so. It never occurs to them that it is their duty to become guardians of their husband's character, as it is the latter's to be guardians of their wives character. And yet what can be plainer than that husband and wife are equal shares of each other's virtues and vices."[12]

The wives can resist the vices of their husbands through non-violent resistance by with drawing all their support direct or indirect from their husband's till they give up their evil ways. But it must be with the motive of love and regard to their husband's and without any tinge of ill-will or hatred. In any way, it should not be for material gain or self-interest, but to make the bond of mutual love and relationship stronger. It may create misunderstanding in the beginning but if it is purely out of love and good will, it is likely to remove all that misunderstanding and bring joy and happiness to their mutual relationships.

Thus, Gandhi attacked the problem of social injustice to women from both the sides—from the side of men who do injustice and from the side of women who have to bear that injustice. He attempted to show to men to free themselves from their sins of injustice to women and at the same time he emphasised the women's freeing themselves from the slavery of customs, whims and fancies of their own and realise their own capacity and strength. He pointed out to them both that their progress and the progress of the country is dependent on the removal of the injustice to the women.

Gandhiji condemned the custom of child marriage in a forthright manner. Writing in 'Young India' in the year 1926, Gandhiji said, "This custom of child marriage is both a moral as well as a physical evil. For it undermines our morals and induces physical degeneration. By countenancing such customs we recede from God as well as Swaraj. A man who has no thought of the tender age of a girl has none of God. And under grown men have no capacity for fighting battles of freedom or having gained it, of retaining it. Fight for Swaraj means no mere political awakening but an all-round awakening-social, educational, moral, economic and political. The practice of early marriage is not confined to any province or class of society, but is practically a universal custom in India and dates from very early time."[13]

Such views of Gandhiji had a profound effect on the public opinion. The people took the issue of child marriage with all sincerity and worked for the removal of the evil. These efforts against child marriage bore fruit in legislative enactment. The central legislative council passed the Child Marriage Restraint Act in the year 1929, known as Sarda Act after the name of its author. According to this Act, the age of consent of for marriage was set at 18 years for boys and 14 years for girls. This Act has been amended from time to time later to raise the age of marriage for girls now to eighteen years and for boys to twenty one years.

Gandhiji repudiated the system of purdha and refuting the charge that it was meant to protect the chastity of women, Gandhiji said, "chastity is not a hot-house growth. It cannot be superimposed. It cannot be protected by the surrounding wall of the purdha. It must grow from within, and to be worth anything it must be capable of withstanding every unsought temptation. It must be as defiant as Sita's.. It must be a very poor thing that cannot stand the gaze of men. Men, to be men, must be able to trust their, womenfolk even as the latter are compelled to trust them."[14]

Gandhiji also made efforts to counteract the practice of prostitution which he called a "life of shame". Gandhiji considered it as his "duty to serve these sisters."[15] To Gandhiji the term "prostitute" applies to woman as well as man who indulges in the act of prostitution. Gandhiji says, "prostitute is commonly supposed to apply to women of lewd character. But the men who indulge in vice are just as much, if not more, prostitutes than the women who, in many instances, have to sell their bodies for the sake of earning a livelihood."[16]

Women and children have a special place in the history of labour legislation in India. The establishment of the International Labour organisation's office in India in the year 1919 influenced considerably the activities of the state in this field and now laws are in force to regulate not only hours of work, but to provide for the health, safety and welfare of women workers. Under the Minimum Wages Act of 1948 the minimum rates of wages payable to persons employed in industries are to be fixed, which are to be the same for both men and women. Under the Factories Act of 1948, separate latrines and washing facilities are to be provided for women. To obviate the dangers arising out of lifting of weights, both under the Factories Acts and the Mines Acts, Government has to fix the maximum load to be lifted by women. Women are also prohibited for employment for pressing cotton in any part of the factory.

Women are employed in large numbers in plantations growing tea, coffee and rubber in Assam, Bengal, Mysore and Madras. Although the law allows working up to 12 hours a day on plantation, employed women generally work for seven to eight hours with a rest interval of about an hour at midday. Women workers are given the additional facility of maternity leave. The earnings of women are, however, lower than that of men.

In case of mine workers there is a ban on their underground employment. The maximum hours of work for women are less than those for men. Under the Mines Act women are prohibited from working between 7 p.m. and 6 a.m. The employment of women in dangerous operations is prohibited.

Besides the women who are engaged either in industries or in professions, there is a vast majority of them who do only household work, are often illiterate and have no training in any profession. To train such women for their gainful employment so that they may supplement the family income and to make them better citizens so that they may take legitimate share in the family, certain welfare programmes have been started after Independence both in the urban as well as rural areas.

There are some separate institutions for female orphans, widows and physically handicapped women. But their management has not been satisfactory. Such institutions need compulsory registration and some grant by the state so that they may work properly.

The State Social Welfare Departments and the Central Social Welfare Board are now rendering financial aid to deserving organisations and institutions working for the welfare of women. According to Planning Commission says that "The Central Social Welfare Board will continue to assist voluntary organisations which implement programmes of women welfare such as condensed courses of education for adult women, urban welfare extension projects, etc. It is proposed to allocate Rs. 1 Crore specially for assisting voluntary organisations for the welfare programmes for destitute women."[17]

The National Council of Women in India was established in 1925 with the object to associate women of all communities in India for the promotion of social, civic, moral and educational welfare of women and children in the country and to co-ordinate the work of national and local organisations in harmony wish these purposes. The activities of the council are carried on by the affiliated state councils and standing sectional committees. These include Child Welfare Work, Village Welfare Work, social education, relief and rehabilitation and emergency relief.

In 1955, the council had 12 branches and was affiliated to the association for moral and social hygiene in India; the Y.W.C.A, Bharat Scouts and Guides and the Trained Nurse's Association. Its headquarters are in New Delhi. All India Women's Conference was establishment in 1929 with the object to work for the welfare of women and children in all ways.

The Kasturba Gandhi Memorial Trust was established in 1945 with the object to conduct and promote such charitable activities as would conduct to the general welfare of the needy women and children in rural areas in India, to establish and maintain welfare institutions for them, to train women workers for rural areas and to promote the welfare of rural women and children in all possible ways. The programme and activities include training of women workers (Gram Sevikas) running of village welfare centers which include children's homes, basic education centers, maternity homes, dispensaries and leprosy relief centers. The trust had 15 branches in the year 1955 to cater to the needs of all.the states in India. There are also small local organisations which provide dispensaries and maternity centers, homes for destitute children and shelter homes for women. They also organise programmes for education, recreation and training in handicrafts.

On the Government side there is need for having separate Social Welfare department and there should be a special section dealing with Women Welfare. At the all India is the Central Social Welfare Board which co-ordinates the activities of the social welfare agencies from the government side, having a separate section for women welfare.

It must be said that in the Gandhian spirit the women in India should not desire to the little in any way those traditions which have in the past contributed to the welfare of the individual and have been the means of raising the dignity of Indian womenhood and conserving the spiritual attributes of the Indian nation.

Education creates a sentiment of self regard in the educated person. Education among women in India has given them chances to improve their personality, to think independently, to choose their careers and their companions of life.

Reference:

(1) Mrs. Desai, M.M., "*Women Welfare*" in *History and Philosophy of Social Work in India* (1961), P. 177

(2) Dr. T.S. Devadoss: *Socio-Ethical and Legal Aspects of Dowry* in Vivekananda Kendra Patrika, August 1973. PP. 78-79

(3) M.K. Gandhi, *Harijan*, February 24, 1940

(4) M.K. Gandhi, *Harijan*, March, 28, 1942

(5) *Young India*, 3-10-1929

(6) *Ibid.* 20-2-1918

(7) *Harijan*, 24-2-1940

(8) *Ibid*, 25-1-1936

(9) *Young India*, 20-2-1918

(10) *Young India*, 8-12-1927

(11) *Harijan*, 31-12-1958

(12) *Op. Cit*, 24-4-1937

(13) *Young India*, August, 26, 1926

(14) *Op. Cit*, 3-2-1921

(15) *Young India*, 15-9-1921

(16) *Harijan*, 15-9-1946

(17) G.R. Madan, *Indian Social Problems* Vol. 2, 1994, P. 127

❑ ❑ ❑

Chapter—VIII

Relevance of Gandhian Thought

In recent years the attention of great scholars has been increasingly drawn towards the dangers that mankind faces in the wake of astounding advance of science and technology. Gulf between the rich and the poor nations are widening. Several commissions and conferences to bring about a peaceful order are witnesses to worsening international climate and, acceleration of tensions and conflicts. Poverty and hunger still prevail while resources are being misutilised for production and disbursement of all types of arms and armaments and the spread of the war psychosis in different countries. Political leadership in different countries is sticking to power by playing upon this sentiment of national security rather than trying to find ways and means to solve the problems of hunger and want and work towards the creation of a new world order which eschews violence and exploitation encourages co-operation amongst individuals, groups and nations, brings about great equality and enables rapid structural changes with active participation of the people.

Prof. J. Tinbergin observes: "With this state of affairs the work of Mahatma Gandhi has in a few years come back to our minds. Almost suddenly we now become aware of the possibility that in respects he may have had messages also for the world of today. In the new light of what we were almost unaware of ten to fifty years ago we shall receive inspiration from what India's great spiritual leader already several decades ago was teaching. In this situation the relevance of Gandhian Thought alone well be able to solve our difficulties on a lasting basis."[1]

Mahatma Gandhi held a unique position in the public life of this country for about five decades as the leader of not only the greatest political movement, but also as a moral and social reformer with an immense and unprecedented following. He had imbibed a rare insight to the various problems facing our country to which others could not. His ideas in economic problems revealed a pragmatic and rational approach specially for the economic problems faced by our country.

In the context of Indian Planning, Gandhiji had not expressed his views, specially in his writings and speeches. However, he wrote extensively in the columns of Young India and Harijan on some pertinent issues which may be relevant to Indian Planning. From his writings which are expressed in a very simple manner, we could not extract a well knit system of Planning for implementation. However, Sri. R.K. Vepa had considered Gandhi as a planner. According to him, "Gandhiji was certainly a Planner but his planning was all embracing."[2]

In designing a strategy for economic development, it is natural for the authorities to compare and contrast with a set of available means of instruments. The whole process of economic development can be described as: let there be means where there were ends. Actually, the planning turns means into ends and means for the process of development. Ever since, 1951, when India launched her First Five Year Plan, the word, "Planning" has become synonymous to the word "development" in the developing countries like India.

The basic objective[3] of planning system in India has been growth with social justice which denotes removal of poverty, decentralisation of economic power, optimum use of scarce resources and removal of regional imbalances. If we look at the past experiences of the various Five Year Plans so far completed in India, we find that we are far behind of our professed objectives. We have never realised the extent of planned growth which has been assured at the beginning of every plan.

Instead of removing poverty, the number of poor multiplied on account of growing unemployment and exploding population. The process of planning considerably failed to raise the standard of living of our countrymen and also to eradicate poverty of the general masses. Ever since the beginning of planning in the country, one of the basic objectives has been the decentralisation of economic power i.e. reduction in equalities of income and wealth. But contrary to this, Gandhiji had observed that, "the present plan of industrialisation and through private hand in allocating increasingly larger and larger shares of scarce capital resources to a small class of capitalist business."[4] This has resulted in the tremendous growth[5] of the big business groups like a Mafat Lal, Shri Ram Thaper and Walchand groups and also of the old groups of Tata, Birla etc. Our planning has failed to curb this monopolistic tendencies. It was correctly pointed out by Mehta that "in spite of the legislation to curb monopolies, nationalisation of banks and more socially oriented, policies of financial institutions, the largest of the corporate groups, for instance, remain in an advantageous position to garner public resources or enlarge business."[6] The existing disparities[7] are perpetuated, and accentuated during the course of planned area of development and had aggravated social and political tensions in the societies.

The relevance of Gandhian ideas, and their Universal applicability is precisely because of the fact that his ideas and thoughts are not based on colonial dominations and exploitative attitudes, cut throat competition, and some other material and worldly values. As against these, they are based on strong human values with moral and spiritual touching. He wanted to give a spiritual touch to all economic, social, political and other problems which he thought as the root cause of all prosperity and happiness. His ideas were always to the best interests and to the real solution of the problem of mankind.

Mahatma Gandhi stood for a simple and, more or less, self-sufficient living in the rural surroundings mainly because he could foresee that a highly sophisticated, and centralised life in the cities would inescapably, lead to the organisation of inhuman violence's and aggressive nationalism resulting in international tensions and wars of unprecedented devastation.

Let us try to examine Gandhi's ideas not in retrospect but in the perspective of the timeless values and virtues for which the Mahatma stood.

It is almost a new civilisation and culture which Mahatma Gandhi has projected. How much of it can be applicable immediately to the present day problems has to be studied and applied. While intellectual understanding is fundamentally necessary, more important is heartful acceptance of approach and will to act accordingly. "My life is my message"[8], observed Gandhi "Life reveals all men and death reveals the eminent". This is true in the case of the Mahatma. Gandhiji's cherished desire was expressed thus: "I wish to wipe every tear from every human eye."[9] He tried to alleviate the sufferings of the sick, the poor and the downtrodden. Inspite of the earnest efforts, he could not succeed to the extent he desired. It was because he lived far ahead of his times and the people could not respond to his mighty moral awakening due to their inherent weakness. It is not necessary to lose hope. Let us have a clear vision of the future of our country and try to understand today the perennial principles of his life-mission.

Gandhiji's precepts of self-sacrifice, devotion to societal aims and application of ethical values to economic welfare will release mass energies for new experiments in social change. Gandhiji has restated and reinterpreted the fundamental principles of Satya, ahimsa and sarvodaya in terms of modern life. His special contribution was to make the concept of ahimsa meaningful in the Socio-Political spheres by moulding tools of non-violent action to use as positive force in the search for the ultimate Truth. Various political scientists economists, sociologists and spiritualists have studied Gandhi's political, economic, social, religious and spiritual concepts. Some of these scholars are of the view that Gandhi's ideas are pragmatic and always relevant with some modifications, irrespective of the time and place. But to some others, Gandhi's ideas are entirely irrelevant and inapplicable in an age of scientific and technological progress with its attendant complexity of issues. Whatever may be the contrary views in this on going debate on Gandhism, one thing is beyond doubt that

Gandhism presents a new, dynamic, revolutionary and rational approach to existing political and socio-economic problems. Shriman Narayan says that "the more I think about diverse problems facing India at present, the more I feel convinced that Gandhian approach alone will be able to solve our difficulties on a lasting basis."[10]

Gandhiji, popularly known as Mahatma Gandhi, holds a unique position in the public life of this country in the new millennium (it is the 21st century) as the leader of not only a great political movement, but as a moral and Social reformer with our immense and unprecedented following. Crores of men and women of different castes, creeds, classes and diverse occupations, in the West as well as in the East, rose to the occasion to the call of his political idealism. He had really identified himself completely with the toiling and poverty stricken masses of India and he lived as the poorest of his country men lived. Gandhiji had, infact, imbibed a rare insight into the various problems facing the country to which others could not.

Gandhi was of the firm opinion that exploitation was the essence of violence as it harmed the personality of individuals. He believed that exploitation became a reality when power was concentrated in a single body like the state. The State represents (says Gandhi) "violence in a concentrated and organised form. The individual has a soul,, but as the state is a soulless machine, it can never be weaned from violence to which it owes its very existence."[11] Destroying individuality means exploitation which led to violence. Therefore to violence and to ensure maximum flowering of the human personality, decentralisation of political power must become an end of a progressive and welfare oriented society. The question arises as to whether this kind of non violence which Gandhi visualised could be search in a reasonable manner in the modern state. Gandhi himself was not sure about it. He believed that "a Government cannot succeed in becoming entirely non-violent, because it represents all the people. I do not today conceive of such a golden age. But I do believe in the possibility of a predominantly non-violent society. And I am working for it."[12]

According to Gandhi, political power of the state was not an end in itself, but "one of the means enabling the people to better their condition in every department of life,"[13] Gandhi saw human progress in human happiness by combining all mental and moral growth."[14] the greatest good of all rather that the greatest good of the greatest number. Gandhi was of the firm opinion that to "what extent the ends were pure. He always said that if the means was proper the ends would take care of themselves."[15] Gandhi's objectives is securing human happiness with full mental and moral growth with the greatest good of all, was a noble goal in itself. Gandhi maintained that such an "end can be achieved under decentralisation. Centralisation as a system is inconsistent with non-violent structure of society."[16]

In Gandhi's concept of village Swaraj every village must have freedom to manage its affairs without external interference from above in its area of competence. It must have its own organisational structure in the form of Government. Gandhi held the view that "the Government of the village will be conducted by the Panchayat of five members, annually elected by the adult villagers, male and female, possessing minimum prescribed qualification... . Since there will be no system of punishment in the accepted sense, this panchayat will be the legislature, judiciary, and executive combined to operate for its year of office. Any village can become such a republic today without much interference even from the present Government.

Gandhian economy is based on Self Sufficiency. "Self-reliance is the basis of freedom while dependence on others is the essence of Slavery."[17] observes J.C. Kumarappa. Gandhi also advocates for "Co-operative economy". Gandhian Thought seeks to build up a society with a bias towards rural civilisation, in which industries would be decentralised and village could be as self-sufficient and possible.

People should imbibe the spirit of Swadeshi, but for the past so many decades people are not imbibing the spirit of Swadeshi. After independence the people forget the value and the spirit of Swadeshi. At least in the new millennium we hope that all people should imbibe the spirit of Swadeshi. We should note that excessive reliance on external aid would ultimately Sap our energies and undermine the spirit of self-help. There can be real green revolution only when the Indian farmer is properly trained in modern farming techniques, and also introduce new innovations in cultivation. The present national plans are bureaucratic nature. It may be suggested that besides the centralised public sector and the private sector, there could be a co-operative sector, a municipal sector and other forms of decentralised ownership and management of industry and trade. All economic and social policies would have to be directed towards the end of securing for everybody the basic necessities of life like food, clothing, shelter, education and health. Although various considerations of economic and technological efficiency have to be kept in view, it should not be forgotten that the human aspects has to be the decisive factor in our schemes of economic planning. Gandhian planning is essentially democratic and humanistic in essence. It is humanistic because its first postulate is to provide employment to all. It is democratic because the fruits of labour and capital are to be shared by all and for the welfare of all. This is the essence of Sarvodaya which still remains an idealised goal of Gandhian thought. To realise it, should be our endeavour.

Gandhiji says, "What I object is the craze for machinery and not machinery as such. The craze is for what they call labour saving machinery. Men go on "saving labour" till thousands are without work and thrown on the open street to die to starvation."[18]

We know that Gandhiji was not against the use of machines or centralisation wherever it was indispensable. He was not opposed to machines as such but he was against making men slaves of machines. He was against it as it concentrates production and distribution in the hands of a few. He very well knew that this body itself is a most dedicated piece of machine. What he objected to was the craze for machine. Gandhiji stated, that I am not against machinery as such, but I am opposed to it when it masters us."[19]

Modern man seems to be attracted by violent technology while non-violent and soft technology repels him. But of late even in the West there is a trend towards intermediate technology and everywhere there is a realisation that labour saving, capital intensive, highly sophisticated technology transfer of mass production has no relevance to the ""Third World where there is plenty of labour, little capital, lack of technical sophistication and elaborate infrastructure.

The most important principles which influenced Gandhi, and which later became the guiding spirit behind all his ideas, was the principle of Sarvodaya – the good of all. This principle originated out of his reading of Ruskin's Unto This Last which held, that the good of individual contained in the good of all. It was Gandhi's desire that the goods should percolate even the last of the socio-economic ladder – the poorest of the poor. Given the goal of Sarvodaya Gandhi was confronted with the question of what kind of economic system the country should evolve for itself. It was in this context that his wider social ideas of Swaraj, truth and non-violence inspired him to evolve an economic system which was consistent with his political and moral philosophy. From the ideas of Swaraj emerged the ideas of Swadeshi and self-sufficiency. And from the principle of truth and non-violence emerged a service of economic ideas like non-exploitation, non-possession, trusteeship, bread-labour and so on. All these ideas which in fact having originated under different contexts, formed the founding pillars of Gandhiji's economic system.

Gandhi believed that the economic good of all lay in adopting the principle of Swadeshi or self-sufficiency. Though Gandhi used the principle of Swadeshi earlier as a political weapon to boycott the foreign goods, particularly of the British, it actually acquired economic overtones gradually. It would be noted that the concept of Swadeshi inculcated gradually in the minds of Indians the imperative and the value of self-sufficiency both at the national and at the local village level. He later used this concept along with the other economic idea viz: decentralisation as a technique of building an economic system which was purely Indian and mass based.

The general consideration of mutual confidence and urge to do good in the economic sphere of the Sarvodaya society, for equality of opportunity and peace, new orientation of economic life is of utmost importance. Gandhi called it economics of non-violence. According to him production in a non-violent society will not be for distant profitable markets. It will be first of all for the "immediate neighbour". He called it Swadeshi. In the domain of economics, Swadeshi means that "one should use only things that are produced by the immediate neighbours and serve those industries by making them efficient and complete where they may be found wanting."[20] He defined Swadeshi article as any article which "subserves the interest of the millions even though the capital and talent are foreign but under effective Indian control."[21] He pleaded strongly for stiff protective duties upon foreign goods in order to nurture national industries. The principle of Swadeshi suggested him the "universalising of Khadi or the spinning wheel to enable the crores of our semi-starved countrymen to live."[22]

Khadi has been conceived as the image of Swadeshi. Khadi has passed through several phases showing its history. From being an antiquararity, it became the symbol of India's non-violent struggle for freedom. In hand spinning Gandhi saw to the psychological and political problems of the nationalist movement.

Furthermore, Khadi was a potent instrument of mass uplift and mass education. The spinning wheel was a divine instrument and one calculated to satisfy the needs of the meanest and humblest of human beings. Gandhi felt that centralisation necessarily leads to the enrichment of violence. Hence in the production and sale of Khadi he wanted decentralisation. This decentralisation leading to the elimination of the control of the All India Spinner's Association would prepare the country for the pursuit of decentralisation in other fields.

Expounding the idea of decentralisation in a Sarvodaya society Vinoba observes: "Decentralisation presupposes a comprehensive all-pervading idea behind the various village industries. In the absence of any such idea, small non centralised industrial units mean merely before the machine age. But they were easily swept off with the first impact of the machine age. Decentralisation will stand on a firm foundation. Not only will it not be blown off, but will disintegrate the machine age itself. The present machine age., In spite of its name, is wholly unlike a machine, being totally controlled machine age. But like all other weapons, the machines too, though invented by man, are inherently non-human. Hence, they cannot be humanised beyond a certain limit. "Since times immemorial villages provided the base for the economic structure of the country while towns produced more sophisticated articles. The industrial structure was thus well diversified and dispersed. It was the British who destroyed not only our glorious trade but also our rural industries for self-interest. The industrial revolution of England thrived at the cost of India while the artisans of the country wiped out from the industrial scene. The basic contradiction of modern industrial civilisation was very well diagnosed by Mahatma Gandhi. The goal of rural urban integration under which land management is better organised to support industrialisation for bridging the productivity gap between rural and urban workers might be an ideal where the cultural fusion between the two societies is complete. Under existing Indian conditions, according to Gandhi, "we shall have to find out whether the villager who produces an article or food stuff rests contents with exporting it and with using a cheap substitute imported from outside. We shall have to see that the villagers become first of all self-contained and then cater to the needs of the city dewellers."[23] Till Gandhiji enunciated his view, villages were looked upon as appendages to the towns, Gandhiji wanted to reverse the process. According to Gandhiji, a healthy economic relationship between town and country implies the fulfillment of the following interrelated conditions:

i) that in the rural economy of his conception cities must find their "natural place" in the economy;

ii) that they must primarily be clearing houses, for the village products;

iii) that the primacy of agriculture, and of industries allied to agriculture in the rural areas should be recognised as the foundation of economic development; and

iv) that the economic relation between town and country must be reciprocally beneficial not exploitative.

What have called the Gandhian approach to economic development has been commanding greater attention, getting much place these days both at the national and international levels. This is possible because the experience of development of different countries of world suggest that something is basically and fundamentally wrong with present approach. The theories and models of economic development have not provided satisfactory solutions to the basic problems of the world economy with the result that the efforts to achieve economic development in terms of material prosperity has created many severe economic and social problems. The energy crisis, the pollution problems, the threatening inflation and unemployment problem, the glaring difference between the poverty of underdeveloped countries and affluence of developed countries, the economic confrontations between these countries and many other such problems have now come to affect the world economy. This is perhaps more true of the Indian economy where even after a lapse of more than 25 years of experience of economic development, we are not even in a position to launch a frontal-attack on the basic issues of our economy—removal of poverty, social and economic inequalities and backwardness, huge unemployment in rural and agricultural economy. Our experiences tell that with all the sophisticated techniques and models of planning.[24] We did not attain much and whatever was achieved had created more problems for us. These reference are sufficient to state that the material approach to economic development so widely followed has not come grips with uneven growth the growing inequality, income distribution and the problems of co-ordination of different sections of the economy.[25] In the present approach we find that all that comes across in terms of trade, commerce, financial arrangements and human attitudes are attempts to continue with the past practices of short term gains of limited groups or communities. These attitudes, structures and arrangements do not provide long term solution to the problems of mankind. It is in this background that Gandhian approach to economic development can be shown to have its relevance in solution of the basic problems of mankind. It is because of this that economic and social policies, attitudes and structures are being revised in almost all countries of the world to make the efforts to economic development more meaningful. It has almost been, universallv realised that the

Gandhian approach to economic development or any such approach like Gandhian for those who do not want to use the name of Gandhiji is the real solution to the problems with which the world economy is concerned. The relevance of Gandhian ideas becomes one more important in the sense that this idea provides a key to the dilemma of the growth process of the contemporary world economy. Somehow we seem to have realised the relevance of the Gandhian approach to economic development but we are not very clear in giving it a practical shape.

In his approach to economic development, Gandhiji was primarily concerned with the development of starving dumb millions, downtrodden and socially economically backward people. He was of the opinion that in order to end the exploitation of the masses political freedom must include real economic freedom.[26] For removing poverty and unemployment Gandhiji thought of the self-sufficient village economy with the development of cottage and small scale industries making use of the potential labour force so abundantly available. He was against large scale industrialisation and indiscriminate use of machines and automations as they were necessarily to deteriorate the conditions of masses. He was in favour of economic decentralisation and for that he wanted to tame the evils of a capitalist economy and thus to bring his own concept of socialism for the development of all irrespective of any distinctions.

If the Gandhian approach for the development of economy on a decentralised way is adopted, it would also need a change in the present system of education and training. Much of the cost of education and training would be reduced considerably and would not go waste as we find it today. Crores of students are wasting their time, energy and money for getting a kind of education which they find to be quite useless. This has been causing great anxiety and frustration for the Student Community. The restlessness of the society of this account is quite marked and politicians with vested interests are taking political advantage out of it. The students are being exploited too for the selfish gains of few. If we make efforts to train the youth of the villages with simple arts and crafts so that they may do something to earn their living by staying in the villages, we would be doing more service to them rather than attracting them in the urban centres with all their glamour and outmoded system of education meant only for making clerks in the offices. We know that simple arts and crafts my be learnt within a few months at much limited cost and time. We should teach them to learn things themselves and understand the intricacies and fineness of the life, their cultural values and a better and decent way of living. They should be explained the importance of dignity of labour, simple living and high thinking. They should be explained about our cultural heritage and how to preserve it. This will also help in heartening the process of decentralisation in the country.

If we do not follow the approach of decentralised development in the country as advocated by Gandhiji, the dignity of man as a man also will be lowered considerably.

Gandhiji conceived and wished the development of our society on the lines of Ram Rajya, where everyone enjoyed life full of happiness and devoid of any ailment physical or otherwise. He thought of a society where every one had equal opportunity to develop equal rights and benefits, as far as possible. He advocated simple life with austerity but with noble thoughts not thinking of "self" alone but sacrificing the "self" for the sake of others. He thought of a society which was self-sufficient economy and where all the necessaries were provided to all and sundry. He took a village, the nerve centre of the country, to be as a unit for the purpose of development and wanted it to be self-sufficient as far as possible. He wanted us all to practice all the virtues, which may be briefly summed up in two virtues i.e., truth and non-violence and shun all which we have branded as sins from time to time. He wanted us to pursue the truth and non-violence with encouragement and conviction in the broadest sense of the terms. For this, he wanted each of us to leave our cowardish mentality and be courageous enough to face the challenges of life boldly. He thought of a society where men and women live together with equal rights without any distinction of class, caste, or creed and where women were not exploited mainly because they were weak.

We find today, as in the past, disparity in the socio-economic structure of our country. On the one hand, we have an affluent class which is living luxuriously and trying to follow the Western way of life. The rich of the country have undoubtedly become richer. On the other hand we have a middle class in our society; struggling for their existence. But in this class also one group has started flourishing, considerably as they are amassing black money by giving up all their moral values. However, the facilities available to lower middle fixed income group have been reduced. Corruption in the society is not only rampant but has become part of life. The poor are becoming poorer and their sufferings have increased considerably. The social structures have not changed on the lines which Gandhiji had thought out. As the policy of the Government planners and the administrators are not going to change considerably in the near future, the prospects of change on Gandhian lines are also quite bleak.

In the new millennium it is our duty and responsibility to train the youth in a proper way to earn their livelihood. The Central Government, the State Government and the voluntary organisation must encourage and train the youth in a proper way so that they can earn their livelihood in a peaceful manner. We must explain the important of dignity of labour, simple living and high thinking. They should be explained about our cultural heritage and how to preserve it without training them to love foreign culture and foreign goods more and more. This will also help in hastening the process of decentralisation in the country.

Shriman Narayan, has gone up to the extent to say with conviction that "instead of being medieval and out-of date Bapu's ideas are even ahead of times and economic and political compulsions would inevitably force us to revert to them for resolving some of the paradoxes that intrigue us today."[27] Prof. Myrdal also thinks solutions of the Indian socio-economic problems in terms of Gandhian ideas but for its implementation as he wrote, "the revolutionary changes in social, economic and political institutions, attitude and practices are separately needed."[28]

To conclude, we can assert that Gandhian ideas of economic development are not the out moded concepts but are essentially rational and scientific concepts and intune with modern economic themes regarding economic development of the developing countries like India Though Gandhiji focussed his attention mostly on the socio-economic problems present in India, but his analysis, vision and strategy bore relevance throughout the globe. But setting aside the world-wide aspect for the movement, even India is apparently no closer to "Swaraj", than it was while under the British. Yet on closer examination, we can see that Gandhiji's work has not come to an end. Gandhiji's ideas, so often rejected, misunderstood, and neglected, are finding their way in the consciousness of the world and they are becoming popular and expanding. It is a movement that aims at nothing less than an ultimate transformation of the world a movement that is not likely to disappear until and unless peace on earth becomes a reality."[29] Thus it becomes quite clear that in the new millennium if the Gandhian ideas are linked up with the broad functioning of our economic planning, we are sure to achieve the objectives of our plans. If the plan of the country is prepared and implemented in the light of the Gandhian concepts giving appropriated priorities to the sectors relevant for developing the standard of life of the masses along with other allied sectors, resolution of the existing socio-economic problems will come nearer to our approach and the nation along with all its glamorous achievements, will be able to solve the basic problems of poverty, unemployment and inequality in the distribution of income and wealth which was the dream of the "Father of the Nation" for independent India. Gandhian ideas was relevant during his life time, continue to be relevant today and shall remain so far many decades to follow.

Reference:

1. Shriman Narayan, "India needs Gandhi", S. Chand and Co., Pvt. Ltd., New Delhi, 1976, P. 2.

2. Vepa R.K., "The Economic Thought of Gandhi", Gandhi Vigyan Journal of the Academy of Gandhian Studies, Vol.1, No.1, October 1977, P. 28.

3. This was professed when planning began in the fifties in our country, Planning Commission, "The First Five Year" Government of India, P. 28.

4. Gadgil, D.R., "The Paths of Planned Economy in India", Akhil Bhartiya Sarva Seva Sangh Prakashan, Varanasi, 1961, P. 41.

5. Singh, Charan, "India's Economic Policy—The Gandhian Blue Print", Vikas Publications, Delhi, P. 73.

6. Mehta B, "Failures of Indian Economy", Chetna Publications, New Delhi, 1974, P. 5.

7. Journal of Gandhian Studies, Gandhian Bhavan, University of Allahabad, 1984, P. 157.

8. Gandhian Thought, University of Madras, March 1981, P. 33.

9. Ibid P. 33.

10. Shriman Narayan, "India Needs Gandhi", S. Chand and Co. Pvt. Ltd., New Delhi, 1976, P.1.

11. The Modern Review, October. 1935, P. 413.

12. Harijan, March 9, 1940, P. 31.

13. Young India, March 2, 1981, P. 5.

14. Harijan, June 18, 1942, P. 5.

15. Harijan, February 11, 1939, P. 8.

16. Harijan, January 18, 1942, P. 5.

17. "Gandhian Thought", University of Madras, March 1981, P. 38.

18. Young India, November 13, 1924, PP-85-86.

19. Harijan, 1937, P. 18.

20. M.K. Gandhi, Speeches and Writings of Mahatma Gandhi, G.A. Natesan and Co., 4th edition; P. 336.

21. M.K. Gandhi, Harijan, February, 25, 1939.

22. M.K. Gandhi, From Yerwada Mandir, Ashram Observances, N.P.H. Ahamadabad, 1945.

23. Mathur and Mathur, Economic Thought of Mahatma Gandhi.

24. P.R. Brahmanand, How will have planned; The Illustracted Weekly of India.

25. John K. Galbraith, The Public Purpose of Economics, the American Reviews, spring 1974, PP. 52-53.

26. Gunnar Myrdal, Asian Drama, Vol.II, P. 723.

27. Sriman Narayan, "Relevance of Gandhian Economics", Journal of Gandhian Studies, Allahabad, Vol. Vo. 17, October, 1977, P. 25.

28. Myrdal, Gunnar, "Poverty, Inequality and Gandhi", Journal of Gandhian Studies, Vol.II, No. 4, July 1975.

29. Shephard, Mark, "Mahatma Gandhi—The Legacy" Gandhi Marg Op. Cit. P. 38.

❑ ❑ ❑

Chapter—IX

Conclusion

India for ages has been the sacred land of people who have shown reverence for spiritual views. India is the Bharata-Sakti the living energy of a great spiritual conception and fidelity to it is the principle of her existence. Swami Vivekananda describes India as 'the blessed Punya-bhumi' and as the land from where came the founders of religions from the ancient times deluging the earth again and again with the pure and perennial waters of spiritual truth.

Gandhi lived, worked and tried to seek solutions to the communal, religious, social, economic and political problems facing the Indian people of the first half of the twentieth century. Gandhiji's ideas and solutions, based mainly on the twin principles of Truth and Non-violence, are however, universal and their application to life is bound to prove beneficial not only to Indian people, but to all the people of the world.

The modern military weapons have become so indiscriminate and their efforts so catastrophic that the very existence of mankind is threatened. Unscrupulous pursuit of material welfare without heading ethical and human values, has eaten into the very vitals of national life and culture. The moral fibre of the people has been weakened. The only practical way to resolve these problems in a lasting manner is to turn once again to the ideals of Mahatma Gandhi, study them in depth and find proper solutions for our ailments. No shadow of doubt can exist that the world needs Gandhiji in the new millennium more than ever before. He is not a relic of the past, but a prophet of the future. In his own words, "So long as my faith burns bright as I hope it will even if I stand alone, I shall be alive in the grave and what is more, speaking from it."[1] Gandhiji's ideas are by no means outmoded as some believe, and, on the contrary might well be applied more often in today's world.

The relevance of Gandhian ideas, and their universal applicability is precisely because of the fact that his ideas and thoughts are not based on colonial dominations and exploitative attitudes, cut throat competition, and some other material and worldly values. As against these they are based on strong human values with moral and spiritual touching. He wanted to give a spiritual touch to all economic, social, political and other problems that he thought as the root cause of all prosperity and happiness. His ideas were always to the best interests and to the real solution of the problems of mankind.

Mahatma Gandhi stood for a simple and more or less, self-sufficient living in the rural surroundings mainly because he could foresee that a highly sophisticated and centralised life in the cities would inescapably lead to the organisation of inhuman violences and aggressive nationalism resulting in international tensions and wars of unprecedented devastation. Gandhiji, therefore, advocated the establishment of ideal villages where the people could pursue the ideal of "Simple living and high thinking." But this ideal has been criticized, ridiculed and even denounced as an opiate to keep the poor quiet and help the present social order to go on.

Prof. Dennish Meadow's is of the opinion that human environment is a shocking way and there is limit to the world material growth and the world economy faces a very gloomy picture in the New Millennium if we do not change radically our present policies. The ever widening gap between rich and poor, worsening economic and political relations, economic imperialism, multinationals and techno-structure are among the more important problems at both the internal and international levels, the solution of which is not becoming possible through the traditional and conventional methods of modern world. With reference to these problems the relevance of Gandhian ideas are very much emphasised by Prof. Tinbergin in the following words: "The rich of the earth should prepare themselves for the simpler life in future. The leading philosophy of the present day society which always asks for more material goods and does not attach much value at simplicity life or modesty in claims has to be replaced by alternative philosophies and surely much could be learned from Mahatma Gandhi's words and example. The real values of life do contain a sufficient quantity of goods and shelter, but it is not necessary to have the luxuries now aimed at. Cultural values will have to be upgraded again.[2]

Gandhiji understood that economic equality is the master key to non-violent independence[3] and hence a very important aspect of his Ramarajya. Gandhiji thought that by a few simple principles some kind of practicable economic equality would be achieved. Gandhiji favoured "Production by the mass" opposed to "mass production". But it is significant that he never opposed machinery as such: what he opposed was craze for machinery.

Gandhiji an apostle of non-violent action never approved war—a violent action. He rejected outright and condemned war as a means of resolving a conflict. According to Gandhi the problem of peace was not just a political problem involving the adjustment or rectification of relations between armed nations. It was the problem of mankind, posing a challenge not only to states but also to every individual human being and human group. He, therefore, endeavoured to establish peace between man and man, group and group and national and nation.

As a realist Gandhiji was prepared to concede that "there might be a world police in the absence of universal belief in non-violence."[4] But this force would be, "a concession to human weakness, not ... an emblem of peace."[5] This would function more as a SHANTI SENA or a PEACE BRIGADE than a modern fighting force. The successful implementation of the Gandhian technique depends on the willingness of the individual to commit himself for the chosen ideal with the attitude of "one step is enough to me." His manner of living will indicate his commitment. What he is and does not without significance. The way to peace lies through peace.

In ancient periods common people were oppressed by arbitrary Governments. They had no rights or status, taxation was arbitrary and individual liberties were not recognised. People clamoured and obtained either peacefully or by force, what may be called political rights. But the masses of the people were still not ensured for a full and contented life and the pursuit of happiness. The state was only concerned with Law and Order and did not restrict individual liberty in many other spheres.

The unrestricted individualism and uncontrolled profit motive as an incentive to all private endeavour were its main features. The emphasis, however, shifted gradually from political rights to social rights and it was opined that certain weaker sections must be protected by the state. Active pursuit of public welfare became the accepted canon of modern political and social philosophy.

There is no state religion in India. It only means that in matters of religion it is neutral. It is the ancient doctrine in India that the state protects all religions but interferes with none.

CASE LAW

Vasudev Vs Vamanji (1881) I.L.R. Bombay 1980. The state can have no religion of its own. It should treat all religion equal in the eyes of Law. The state does not identify with any particular form of religion but gives equal protection to all forms. The state must extend similar treatment to the Church, the Mosque and the Temple.

Fundamental rights are guaranteed by the Indian Constitution. In the present context "Social legislation has to concern itself with the promotion of the welfare of individuals and groups. Legislation should be so designed as to invest the life of everyone with a purpose and with the means and opportunities for the fulfillment of the hopes and aspirations of the average citizens in the light of our constitution."[6] The State has to promote the welfare of all (Sarvodaya) but with declared bias in favour of the needy, neglected and weaker sections of the people.

The main function of legislation is to provide, protect and

promote a framework of social regulation with in which the individual citizen can pursue his several notions of what makes for his happiness. Gandhiji conceived and wished the development of our society on the lines of Ram Rajya, where everyone enjoyed life full of happiness and devoid of any ailment—physical or otherwise. He thought of a society where everyone had equal opportunity to develop equal rights and benefits, as far as possible. He advocated simple life with austerity but with noble thoughts not thinking of "Self" alone but sacrificing the "Self" for the sake of others. He thought of a society which was Self-sufficient economy and where all the necessaries were provided to all and sundry. He took a village, the nerve center of the country, to be as a unit for the purpose of development and wanted it to be self-sufficient as far as possible. He wanted us all to practice all the virtues, which may be briefly summed up in two virtues, i.e., truth and non-violence and shun all that we have branded as 'sins' from time to time. He wanted us to pursue the truth and non-violence with encouragement and conviction in the broadest sense of the terms. For this he wanted each of us to leave our cowardish mentality and be courageous enough to face the challenges of life boldly. He thought of a society where men and women live together with equal rights without any distinction of class, caste or creed and where women were not exploited mainly because they were weak.

(1) Have we ever thought to develop our society on Gandhian lines?

(2) Are we really moving in that direction?

(3) Are we thinking on those lines and trying to help the masses?

(4) Are our leaders or rulers leading us in this direction?

(5) Do we have equality of opportunity available to all the countrymen?

(6) Are the rich classes of the society or businessmen following the concept of trusteeship in practice?

(7) Do we find morality, virtues, good values etc., being

practised by us and are they reigning supreme over the vices and sins?

(8) De we have that kind of economic thinking or policies as were advocated by Gandhiji which would have been most beneficial for the teeming masses living in poverty?

If we think deeply and at the socio-economic structure of our society we would, in fact, not get the answers to the above questions in the affirmative. Changes in socio-economic structure of our country since more than five decades are not in those directions as visualised or advocated by Gandhiji.

We find today, as in the past, duality in the socio-economic structure of our country. On the one hand, we have an affluent class that is living luxuriously and trying to follow the western way of life. The rich of the country have, undoubtedly become richer. On the other hand, we have a middle class in our society, struggling for their existence. But in this class also one group has started flourishing considerably as they are amassing black money losing all their moral values and trying to initiate the rich class of society. However, the facilities available to lower middle fixed income group have been reduced. Corruption in the society is not only rampant but has become part of life. The poor are becoming poorer and their sufferings have increased considerably. The social structures have not changed on the lines, which Gandhiji had thought of.

Gandhiji fought against untouchability, casteism, drinking and other social evils in his lifetime and showed the ways in which such problems can really be solved. However, even after more than five decades the situation has not improved. At least in the New Millennium the situation should improve as per Gandhian lines.

Every now and then, we listen of exploitation of scheduled caste and backward class people. Prohibition has not been successful and number of persons who drink, has been increasing year after year. Communal harmony at the alter of which Gandhiji sacrificed his life is still a dream. Today, we find that communal disturbances have been taking place in the country now and then.

From this point shall we also change as desired by Gandhiji has not taken place. At least in the new Millennium change as desired by Gandhiji may take place.

We find the impact of hippy cult, Jeans, Pop culture, Disco, Five star culture etc., on the minds of the youth of the country. Those who are educated find themselves completely alienated from the common man. We have become more and more materialistic in our approach and we are multiplying our wants day-by-day. The idea of self-sacrifice or wantlessness or say minimisation of wants is not the talk of the day in the society. One basic premise, which Gandhiji enunciated, was the need for restriction of wants. Gandhiji pointed out that "we are not always aware of our real needs and most of us improperly multiply our wants and thus unconsciously, make thieves of ourselves."[7] There is no doubt that since Gandhiji's time the craze for material goods has intensified and India too has been infected with it. This produces visible disparities between the rich and the poor and leads to social discord between the two. In this connection we can quote Sir Julian Huxley, who pointed out that "Like population explosion, the consumption explosion cannot continue much longer; it is an inherently self-defeating process. Sooner, rather than, later; it is an inherently self-defeating process. Sooner, rather than later, we shall be forced to get away from a system based on artificially increasing the number of human wants and set about constructing one aimed at the qualitative satisfaction of real human needs—spiritual and mental, as well as material and psychological.[8] But what we find today is that there is a mad race for more and more goods not only in the urban areas but also in the rural areas.

No man in India has done more than Gandhi in recent times for the elevation of women and the occupation by them of their rightful place in domestic and public life. A passionate lover of humanity, an implacable foe of injustice in whatever form or sphere, it is small wonder that Gandhiji early espoused the woman's cause. Throughout his long life of service, Gandhiji preached forcefully against the wrongs done to women in the name of law, tradition and even religion. He has spoken out fearlessly against enforced widowhood, purdha, the dedication of girls to temples, prostitution, early marriage, dowry system, the economic bondage and material slavery of women.[9] Gandhiji championed the cause of women. He considered woman as the incarnation of ahimsa. Ahimsa means infinite love , which again means infinite capacity for suffering. When women, the mother of man, shows this capacity in the largest measure? ... . Let her forget she ever was or can be the object of man's lust. And she will occupy her proud position by the side of man as his mother, maker and silent leader. It is given to her to teach the art of peace to the warring world thirsting for that nectar.[10]

Gandhiji, in short, considered women as "the personification of self-sacrifice." Gandhi was against the purdha system. Gandhiji wrote: "Chastity is not a hot-house growth. It cannot be protected by the surrounding wall of the purdha. It must grow from within, and to be worth anything, it must be capable of withstanding every unsought temptation... . The real purdha is of the heart. A women who peeps through the purdha and contemplates a male on whom her gaze falls, violates the spirit behind it. If a woman observes it in spirit, she is truly carrying out what the great Prophet has said."[11]

Gandhiji considered that "marriage is a natural thing in life, and to consider it derogatory in any sense is wholly wrong. The ideal is to look upon marriage as a sacrament and therefore to lead a life of self-restraint in the married state."[12] Gandhiji was as much a friend of children as of older people. They instinctively saw the light of love in his eyes and were attracted to him. About Kanyadan, Gandhiji says, "What is Kanyadan in the case of little children? Has a father any rights of property over his children? He is their protector, not owner"... . The father forfeits the privilege of protecting when he abuses it by seeking to barter away the liberty of the ward.[13] Thanks to the modern legislators for their wisdom in declaring such marriages as null and void by the enactment of the Special Marriage Act 43 of 1954 and the Hindu Marriage Act 25 of 1955 which curb these social evils including dowry. Here is Gandhiji's advice: "Any young man who makes dowry a condition of marriage discredits his education and his country and dishonours womanhood. The parents should so educate their daughters that they would refuse to marry a young man who wanted a price for marrying."[14]

The legislators in India has adopted certain conditions for a valid marriage and it becomes as an Act. By Section 5 of the Hindu Marriage Act, 1955, a marriage may be solemnised by any two Hindus if the following conditions are fulfilled:

(1) Neither party has a spouse living at the time of the marriage.

(2) At the time of marriage, neither party:

  (a) is inacapable of giving a valid consent to it in consequence of unsoundness of mind; or

  (b) through capable of giving a valid consent has been suffering from mental disorder of such an extent as to be unfit for marriage and the procreation of children; or

  (c) has been subject to recurrent attacks of insanity or epilepsy.

(3) The bridegroom has completed the age of 21 years and the bride the age of 18 years at the time of the marriage.

(4) The parties are not within the degrees of prohibited relationship, unless the custom or usage governing each of them permits of a marriage between the two.

(5) The parties are not sapindas of each other, unless the custom or usage governing each of them, permits of a marriage between the two.

As per the Hindu Marriage Act makes monogamy obligatory for Hindus. Violation of this condition makes the intended marriage null and void and also leads to penal consequences. Under Section 11 a declaration of nullity can be obtained by either party to the marriage. By section 17 of the provisions of Sections 494 and 495 of the Indian Penal Code are made applicable to cases of bigamy. Under Section 494 of the Indian Penal code it is an offence punishable with imprisonment for a term which may extend to 7 years and shall also be liable to fine. Under Section 495 of the Indian Penal Code if the fact of the early marriage was concealed from the spouse it is punishable with imprisonment for a term which may extend to ten years (10 years) and shall also be liable to fine.

In the Hindu marriage Act 1955 Section 5, (ii) provides that neither party is an idot or a lunatic at the time of the marriage. By the amendment in 1976 this provision was completely replaced by three sub-clauses as follows:

(a) In capacity to give a valid consent to the marriage.

(b) Mental disorder making one unfit for marriage and procreation.

(c) Recurrent attacks of insanity.

Violation of this condition makes the marriage voidable at the option of either party and may be annulled by a decree of nullity under Section 12 (1) (b).

The Marriage Act of 1955 prescribes the age limit for marriage. From October 1, 1978, the Age is 21 for men and 18 for women. From May 18, 1955 to September 30, 1978, the age prescribed was 15 for girls and 18 for boys. In the case of girls below the age of 18, the consent of the guardian in marriage was essential.

Every person who procures a marriage of himself or herself to be solemnised under the Act in contravention of the prescribed age rule is made punishable under Section 18. The punishment is simple imprisonment which may extend to 15 days or with fine which may extend to Rs. 1000/- or with both.

The Dowry Prohibition Act was enacted to prohibit the giving or taking of dowry. It extends to the whole of India except the State of Jammu and Kashmir. The Dowry Prohibition Act came into force on 1st July 1961.

As per Section 2 "dowry" means any property or valuable security given or agreed to be given either directly or indirectly by one party to a marriage to the other party to the marriage or by any other persons to either party to the marriage or to any other person at or before or any time after the marriage in connection with the marriage of the said parties. It does not include dower or mahr in the case of persons to whom the Muslim personal law applies.

CASE LAWS

In Madhu Sudan Malhotra Vs Kishore Chandra Bhandari (1988 (36) B.L.J.R. (S.C.) 360, it was held that the furnishing of list of ornaments and other household articles such as refrigerator, furniture, electric appliances etc., at the time of the settlement of the marriage amounts to dowry within the meaning of Section 2.

Section 4 contains the provisions to impose penalties. If any person after the commencement of the Act, gives or takes or bets the giving or taking of dowry he shall be punishable with imprisonment for a term which shall not be less than 5 years and with fine which shall not be less than Rs. 15,000/- or the amount of the value of such dowry whichever is more.

By Section 4A if any person offers through any advertisement in any newspaper, periodical, journal or through any other media any share in his property or any money or both as a share in any business or other interest as consideration for the marriage of his son or daughter or any other relative or prints or publishes or circulates any advertisement relating to the offer shall be punishable with imprisonment for a term which shall not be less than 6 months but which may extend to 5 years or with fine which may extend to Rs. 15,000/-.

As per Section 14 prescribes that whenever a marriage is solemnised under the Act, the Marriage officer shall enter a certificate thereof in the prescribed form in a book called "The Marriage Certificate Book". Such certificate shall be signed by the parties to the marriage and the three witnesses. The certificate shall be deemed to be conclusive evidence of the fact that a marriage under the Act has been solemnised. A marriage solemnised in the manner provided in the Act shall be good and valid in law in India.

The Family Court Act was passed in 1984. It provides for setting up family Courts to deal with disputes related to marriage and family affairs. The Commission of Sati (Prevention) Act was passed in 1987 to prevent the pernicious practice of commission of Sati and its glorification.

The suppression of Immoral Traffic in Women and Girls Act, 1956 was amended in 1986 and was remanded as the Immoral Traffic (Prevention) Act. It was applicable to both the sexes. The detention of a woman for purposes of prostitution is now punishable with a minimum of 7 years Imprisonment. Similarly, stringent punishment was to be awarded to those procuring children for prostitution.

Problems in regard to decentralised system of production, restriction on wants, proper distribution, industrialism, mechanisation of man, minimum wage, role of trade unionism, economic equality, relationship with land lord and peasant, capital and labour and other allied economic problems—all these find a solution in the all comprehensive Gandhian principles of economics, viz., Sarvodaya which aims at the Welfare of all.

The relevance and the application of Gandhian ideas to the present problems of our economy and economic planning has become particularly more significant today with the objective of attaining social justice, eradication of poverty, unemployment, reducing of social and economic inequalities, creating better opportunities for the weaker sections of the society, the small farmers and the landless labourers.

The modern world is primarily governed by two important aspects of power. One is technological power and the other is the power of human relations. Both are fundamental and are imparting greater influence upon the minds of man. Needless to say that among the virtues that have been cultivated since ages, the power of non-violence is supreme. And when the technological power has started using violence as an instrument of total annihilation of mankind then power of non-violence has started gaining momentum in the mind of civilised man. Gandhiji said, "My daily experience, as of those who are working with me, is that every problem would lend itself to solution if we are determined to make the Law of Truth and Non-Violence the Law of life. For Truth and Non-Violence are, to me two faces of the same coin."[15]

In the New Millennium Gandhiji came like a powerful current of fresh air that made us stretch ourselves and take deep breaths, like a beam of light that pierced that darkness and removing all evils which can be compared to like a whirlwind that upset many things but most of all the working of people's mind. In the New Millennium if we are able to live according to the ideals of Mahatma Gandhi, we may be sure that his country of ours will survive, as it has survived for centuries, for many more centuries and its philosophy will make a healing of nations and bringing of people together.

"The Banyan Tree

Has spread its root

As months have turned to years

The day of joy

No room now for tears

Let bells now chime

They do announce

The New Millennium is here."

The shining beacon lights of Mahatma Gandhi's teachings, His principles, Ideas shine to mark the New Millennium.

"Asato mā sad gamaya

Tama so mā jyotir gamaya

Mṛtyor mā amrtam gamaya."

Lead me from the unreal to the real

Lead me from darkness to light

Lead me from death to eternal life.

Raghupathi Ragava Raja Ram

Pathitha Pavana Sita Ram

Eaṣwar Allah Tere Nam

Sabco Sanmati De Bhagavan

Rama Rama Jaya Raja Ram

Rama Rama Jaya Sita Ram.

May the life and teachings of Mahatma Gandhi be a beacon of hope and courage to all of us.

Reference:

(1) *Journal of Gandhian Studies*, Gandhian Bhavan University of Allahabad, P. 101

(2) Jan Tinbergin, *Limit to Growth*, The economic Times, Annual 1972

(3) *Journal of Gandhian Studies*, University of Allahabad, P. 95

(4) *Ibid* - P. 107

(5) *Ibid* - P. 107

(6) Sastri V.V., *Op. Cit.* P. 588

(7) *Journal of Gandhian Studies* (July 1981) P. 254

(8) *Ibid*

(9) Dr. T.S. Devadoss: *Socio-ethical and Legal Aspects of Dowry* in Vivekananda Kendra Patrika, August 1973, PP 78-79

(10) M.K. Gandhi, *Harijan*, Feb. 24, 1940

(11) M.K. Gandhi, *Harijan*, March 23, 1947

(12) M.K. Gandhi, *Harijan*, March 28, 1942

(13) M.K. Gandhi, *Harijan*, June 1, 1928

(14) M.K. Gandhi, *Harijan*, June 1, 1928

(15) *Young India*, 1-10-1931, P. 287

❑ ❑ ❑

Select Bibliography

Agarwal. S.N., *Gandhian Constitution for Free India,* Kitabistan, (Allahabad, 1946)

Aiyangar, K.V.R., *Some Aspects of Ancient Indian Policy,* (Madras, 1935).

Aiyar S.P., *Modernisation of Traditional Society and other Essays,* Macmillan, (Delhi, 1973)

Alexander, Harace, *Social and Political Ideas of Mahatma Gandhi,* (New Delhi, 1949).

Andrews, C.F., *Mahatma Gandhi's Ideas,* (New York, 1930)

Anstey, Vera; *The Economic Development of India,* Longmans Green and Co., 1946.

Appa Saheb Pat Wardhan, *Towards a New Society;* A.B.S.S.S. (Varanasi, 1959).

Baig Tara Ali (ed) *The Woman of India,* Government of India, New Delhi, 1958.

Bandyopodhya, N.C. *Development of Hindu Polity and Political Theories* (Calcutta: 1927)

Barker, Ernest; *Principles of Social and Political Theory* (Oxford University Press, London: 1965)

Behari, Bepin; *Gandhian Economic Philosophy,* Vora and Co., (Bombay, 1963).

Belshaw, C.E., *Traditional Exchange and Modern Markets,* (New Jersy: Englewood Cliffs Prentice Hall, Inc: 1965)

Benn, S.I. and Peters, R.S., *Social Principles and the Democratic State*, George Allen and Unvin Ltd., (London, 1958).

Bhave, Acharya Vinoba; *Democratic Values*, S.S.S. (Varanasi, 1962).

Bhave, Acharya Vinoba; *From Bhoodan to Gramdan*, S.P. (Tanjore, 1967)

Bhave, Acharya Vinoba; *Gramdan – Villagism of Land*, S.P. (Tanjore, 1968)

Bhave, Acharya Vinoba; *Sarvodaya and Communism*, S.P. (Tanjore, 1957)

Bondurant, J.V., *Conquest of Violence: The Gandhian Philosophy of Conflict*, Princeton University Press, (Princeton, J.N. 1958).

Bonsanquet, Bernard: *The Philosophy Theory of the State*, Macmillan and Co., Ltd., (London, 1958)

Bose, Nirmal Kumar: *Selections from Gandhi*, N.P.H. (Ahmedabad: 1948)

Bose, Nirmal Kumar; *Studies in Gandhism*, Merit Publisher, (Calcutta, 1962).

Bowles, Chester; *Ideas, People and Peace* (Bombay: 1961)

Bradley, F.H., *Ethical Studies* (London: 1876)

Buch, M.A; *The Development of Contemporary Indian Political Thought*, Good Companions, Baroda, 1939, Vols. I, II & III)

Burgess, E.W., *The Family* (New York: Litton Educational Publishing, 1963)

Carcus, D.P., *The Nature of the State* (Chicago: The Open Court Publishing Company, 1894)

Catlin, George, *In the Path of Mahatma Gandhi* (Chicago: 1950)

Chakravarthy, Amia, *Mahatma Gandhi and the Modern World*, Calcutta: Modern Book House, 1945)

Char, Narasimha: *A Day Book of Thoughts from Mahatma Gandhi*, (Macmillan, 1969)

Chari, C.T.K. *Some issues about Social Change*, (University of Madras, 1973).

Chatterjee, B.B.,*Gramdan and People* (S.S.S.P. Varanasi, 1969).

Chattopadhyay, Kamala Devi, *Mahatma Gandhi 100 years,* (New Delhi: Gandhi Peace Foundation, 1968).

Cobban, Alfred,*Rousseau and the Modern State* (London: 1934)

Cooley, C.H., *Human Nature and the Social Order* (New York: Charles Seribner's Sons, 1922).

Datta Bhabatosh, *Indian Economic Thought,* (Tata Macgraw, New Delhi, 1978)

Datta, D.M. *The Philosophy of Mahatma Gandhi* (Madison: The University of Wisconsin Press, 1953)

Davies, Kingsley, *Human Society* (New York: The Macmillan company, 1970)

Daya Krishna, *Social Philosophy*—Past and Future, (Simla: Indian Institute for Advanced Study, 1968)

Dayananda, *Light of Truth* (Allahabad: 1915)

Deininger, Whitaker T: *Problems in Social and Political Thought,* Macmillan (London, 1965)

Desai, Mahadev, *Gandhi in Indian Villages* (Ahmedabad: Navajivan)

Desai, Mahadev: *The Gita according to Gandhi*

Devanesan, Chandran D.S. *The Making of the Mahatma,* (Madras: Oriental Longmans, 1969)

Devadoss T.S., *Sarvodaya and the Problem of Political Sovereignty* (Madras: University of Madras, 1974)

Dhawan, Gopinath, *The Political Philosophy of Mahatma Gandhi,* N.P.H. (Ahmedabad: 1951)

Diwakar, R.R. *Mahatma Gandhi 100 years (New Delhi:* Gandhi Peace Foundation, 1968)

Eaton, Jeanette: *Gandhi: Fighter without a Sword,* New York, 1950.

Edwards, Paul: *The Encyclopaedia of Philosophy,* The Macmillan Company, New York, 1967.

Ellwood, Charles. A; *A History of Social Philosophy*, Princeton Hall, New York, 1938.

Fischer, Louis, The Life of Mahatma Gandhi (London: Jonathan Cape, 1951)

Fischer, Louis, Gandhi: His Life and Message for the World (New York, 1954)

Gandhi, Indira, *The Years of Challenge*, (New Delhi: Publications Division, 1973)

Gandhi Kanu, *Swaraj through Charkha* (Sevagram: 1945)

Gandhi, M.K. *Basic Education*, N.P.H. (Ahmedabad: 1951)

Gandhi, M.K. *Communal Unity*, N.P.H. (Ahmedabad: 1949)

Gandhi, M.K. *Constructive Programme*, N.P.H. (Ahmedabad: 1945)

Gandhi, M.K. *Hind Swaraj or Indian Home Rule*, N.P.H. (Ahmedabad: 1939)

Gandhi M.K. *Harijan, N.P.H.*, Ahmedabad.

Gandhi, M.K. *India of My Dreams*, N.P.H., Ahmedabad, 1958.

Gandhi, M.K. *Non-Violence in Peace and War*, N.P.H. (Ahmedabad: Parts 1 & II, 1945)

Gandhi, M.K. *Rebuilding our Villages*, N.P.H. (Ahmedabad: 1952)

Gandhi, M.K. *Sarvodaya*, N.P.H. (Ahmedabad: 1951)

Gandhi, M.K. *Satyagraha*, N.P.H. (Ahmedabad: 1951)

Gandhi M.K. *Towards New Education*, N.P.H. Ahmedabad.

Gandhi, M.K. *Towards Non-Violent Socialism*, N.P.H. (Ahmedabad: 1951)

Gandhi, M.K. *Varnashrama Dharma*, N.P.H. (Ahmedabad: 1962)

Gandhi M.K. *Women and Social Injustice*, N.P.H. (Ahmedabad, 1942)

Gandhi M.K. *In Search of the Supreme*, N.P.H. (Ahmedabad, 1951).

Ganguli B.N., *Gandhi's Social Philosophy* (Delhi: Vikas Publishing House, 1973)

Gregg, R.B. *A Philosophy of Economic Development,* N.P.H. (Ahmedabad)

Gregg Richard, B., *A Philosophy of Indian Economic Development,* N.P.H. (Ahmedabad, 1958)

Gupta, Shanti, S., *The Economy Philosophy of Mahatma Gandhi,* Ashok Publishing House, (New Delhi)

Hacker, Andrew, *Political Theory: Philosophy,* Ideology, Science (New York: The Macmillan Company Ltd., 1961)

Hegel, G.W.F., *The Philosophy of Right,* translated by S.W. Dyde, (London: 1896)

Heim Sath, Charles, H. *Indian Nationalism and Hindu Social Reform* (New Jersey: Princeton, 1964)

Hertzler, *American Social Institutions,* 1961.

Horace, Alexander and others., *Social and Political ideas of Mahatma Gandhi.*

Hunt Elgin, F. *Social Science,* Macmillan (New York, 1972)

Inkeles, Alex, "*Modernisation of Man*" in Myron Weiner (ed., Modernisation: The Dynamic of Growth (Madras: Voice of America Forum Lectures, Study Circle Reprints, Higginbothams (P) Ltd., 1967).

Kapadia, K.M. *Marriage and Family in India* (Oxford University Press, 1968)

Karan Singh, *Prophet of Indian Nationalism* (London: George Allen and Unwin Ltd., 1963)

Kela Bhagavan Das: *Bhoodan, Shramdan, Jeevandan, Bharatiya Grandhamala* (Allahabad, 1955)

Kripalani J.B. *Gandhian Thought,* Orient Longmans (Calcutta, 1961)

Kripalani J.B. *Planning and Sarvodaya,* S.S.S.P. (Varanasi, 1957)

Kripalani J.B. *Towards Sarvodaya,* Kisan Mazdoor Praja Party, (New Delhi, 1951)

Kumarappa, Bharatan: *Capitalism, Socialism or Villagism?* S.S.S. (Varanasi, 1965)

Kumarappa J.C. *Economy of Permanence,* S.S.S. (Varanasi, 1962)

Kumarappa J.C. *Gandhian Economic Thought* S.S.S. (Varanasi, 1962)

Kumarappa J.C. *Gandhian Way of Life,* A.I.V.I.A. (Wardha, 1949)

Kumarappa .J.C. *The Non-Violent Economy and World Peace,* S.S.S. (Varanasi, 1958)

Lanza Delvasto, J.J. *Gandhi to Vinoba*: Rider, (London, 1956)

Lerner Daniel, *The Passing of Traditional Society,* The Free Press of Glencoe (Illinois, 1958)

Mac Iver, R.M. *The Modern State,* Oxford University Press (London, 1966)

Mackenzie Brown: *Traditions of Leadership and Political Institutions in India,* Princeton (New Jersey, 1959)

Maha Devan, T.M.P., *Outlines of Hinduism* (Bombay: Chetana Ltd., 1960)

Mashruwala, K.G. *A Vision of Future India,* N.P.H. (Ahmedabad, 1953)

Mashruwala, K.G. *Gandhi and Marx,* N.P.H. (Ahmedabad, 1956)

Mashruwala, K.G. *Practical Non-Violence,* N.P.H. (Ahmedabad, 1954)

Mathur J.S. *Industrial Civilisation and Gandhian Economics,* Pustakayam, (Allahabad, 1971)

Mehta V., *Social Theory and Political Thought of Sarvodaya,* Laski Institute (Ahmedabad)

Mehta V.L., Decentralised Economic Development, Khadi and Village Industries, Compilation, (Bombay, 1964)

Merton R., *Social Theory and Social Structure,* (Glencoe: Free Press, 1947)

Misra, B.R., Vinoba: *The Economics of Bhoodan Movement,* Orient Longmans, (Calcutta, 1956)

Misra R.N., *Bhoodan Movement in India*, S. Chand and Co., (New Delhi, 1972).

Motwani, Kewal, Manu: *A Study in Hindu Social Theory* (India, Madras: Ganesh and Company, 1934)

Moore, Wilbert E., *Social Change* (New Delhi: Prentice—Hall of India, Second Edition, 1975)

Mukerjee, Hiren., *Gandhi, A Study* (Peoples Publishing)

Mukerjee, Rudhakamol, *The Social Structure of Values*, Macmillan and Co., (London, 1949)

Nag. Kalidas: *Tolstoy and Gandhi*, Pustak Bhandar (Patna, 1950)

Narayan, Jaya Prakash, *From Socialism to Sarvodaya*, S.S.S.P. (Varanasi: 1959)

Narayan, Jayaprakash, *Fundamental Problems of Panchayat Raj* (New Delhi: All India Panchayat Parishad, 1964)

Narayan, Jayaprakash, *Socialism, Sarvodaya and Democracy*, A.P.H. (Bombay: 1964)

Narayan, Jayaprakash, "Gandhi, Vinoba and the Bhudan Movement", S.S.S.P., (Varanasi, 1959)

Narayan, Jayaprakash, *Swaraj for the people*, S.S.S.P., (Varanasi, 1961)

Narayan, Shriman, *Principles of Gandhian Planning*, Kitab Mahal, (Allahabad, 1960)

Narayan, Shriman, *Relevance of Gandhian Economics*, N.P.H., (Ahmedabad, 1970)

Nehru, Jawaharlal, *Mahatma Gandhi*, A.P.H. (New Delhi, 1949)

Nye, F.I. Values, *Family and Changing Society*, 1967)

Ommen, T.K., *Christmatic Movements and Social Change: An Analysis of Bhoodan- Gramdan Movement in India*, University of Poona (Poona, 1967)

Parson Talcott, *The Social System* (Glencoe: The Free Press, 1951)

Prasad, Bimla (Ed.) *Socialism, Sarvodaya and Democracy*, Selected

Work of N.P. Narayanan, A.P.H. (New Delhi, 1964).

Pyarelal, *Gandhian Techniques in the Modern World,* N.P.H. (Ahmedabad, 1959)

Pyarelal, *Mahatma Gandhi: The Early Phase,* 2 Vol. N.P.H (Ahmedabad 1966)

Pyarelal, *Mahatma Gandhi: The Last Phase,* 2 Vols. N.P.H. (Ahmedabad, 1959)

Radhakrishnan S., *An Idealist View of Life,* George Allen and Unwin Ltd., (London, 1952)

Radhakrishnan S., *Freedom and Culture,* G.A. Natesan and Co., (Madras, 1936)

Radhakrishnan S., *Religion and Society,* George Allen and Unwin Ltd., (London, 1956)

Radhakrishnan S., *The Hindu View of Life,* George Allen and Unwin Ltd., (London, 1949)

Radhakrishnan S., *Mahatma Gandhi, Essays and Reflections,* Jaico Publishing House, (Bombay, 1956)

Ranadive, B.T., *Sarvodaya and Communism,* Party Publication (New Delhi, 1958)

Rao, V.K.R.V., Gandhian Alternative to Western Socialism, B.V.B. (Bombay, 1971)

Ray, Benoy Gopal, *Gandhian Ethics,* Navajivan, 1950.

Reddy, V. Narayan Karan, *Sarvodaya Ideology and Acharya Vinoba Bhave, A.P., Sarvodaya Mandal,* (Hyderabad, 1963)

Rolland Romain, *Mahatma Gandhi* (New York, 1924)

Ropkem, Wilhelm, *Humane Economy,* (London, 1961)

Ruskin, J., *Unto this Last,* Smith Elder, (London, 1962)

Sayi Yidain, K.G., *Significance of Gandhi as a Man and Thinker,* P.D., (New Delhi, 1970)

Santhanam, K. *Satyagraha and the State,* A.P.H. (Bombay 1960).

Schumacher, E.F., *Roots of Economic Growth*, The Gandhian Institute of Studies, 1962.

Schumacher, E.F., *Small is Beautiful* (1975), Abucus, Sphere Book Ltd., London.

Sen, Mankumar., *Gandhian Way and the Bhoodan Movement*, S.S.S. (Varanasi, 1964).

Sen, M. (ed.), *The Economic Aspects of Sarvodaya*, Proceedings of the Calcutta Seminar, S.S.S.P. (Varanasi, 1959).

Shukla, C., *Gandhi's View of Life*, B.V.B., (Bombay 1951)

Sitaramayya, B.P., *Gandhi and Gandhism* Vols. I, II, Kitabistan, Allahabad.

Tagore, Rabindranath., *Nationalism*, Mac Millan and Co., (London, 1950)

Tondon Viswanath, *Sarvodaya after Gandhi*, S.S.S. (Varanasi, 1965)

Tendulkar, D.G.*Gandhiji – His Life and Work*. Bombay, 1944)

Varma, V.P. *The Political Philosophy of Mahatma Gandhi and Sarvodaya*, Lakshmi Narain Agarwal (Agra, 1959)

Weldon, T.D., *States and Morals – A Study in Political Conflicts* (London, 1946)

Wellock, Wilfred, *Gandhi as Social Revolutionary*, Orchard Lea, (New Longton, Preston, England)

Willoughby, *The Ethical Basis of Political Authority*, The MacMillan Company, (New York, 1930)

Zachner, R.C., *Hinduism*, Oxford University Press, (1962)

Index